THE SUPREME COURT AND CONGRESS

The Supreme Court in American Life
Samuel Krislov, General Editor

Samuel Krislov, *The Supreme Court and Political Freedom*
Arthur Selwyn Miller, *The Supreme Court and American Capitalism*
Martin Shapiro, *The Supreme Court and Administrative Agencies*
Robert Scigliano, *The Supreme Court and the Presidency*
John Schmidhauser and Larry Berg, *The Supreme Court and Congress*

THE SUPREME COURT AND CONGRESS

Conflict and Interaction, 1945–1968

by

John R. Schmidhauser
University of Iowa

and

Larry L. Berg
University of Southern California

THE FREE PRESS · New York
Collier-Macmillan Limited · London

The Free Press
A Division of The Macmillan Company
866 Third Avenue, New York, New York 10022

Collier-Macmillan Canada Ltd., Toronto, Ontario

Library of Congress Catalog Card Number:
77-160068

printing number
1 2 3 4 5 6 7 8 9 10

Acknowledgements

Portions of Chapter 4 originally comprised part of a chapter entitled "Age and Judicial Behavior: American Higher Appellate Judges," in Wilma Donahue and Clark Tibbitts, *Politics of Age* (Ann Arbor: Institute of Gerontology, 1962); it is reproduced with permission. A condensed version of the roll call analysis in Chapter 7 appeared in the Spring 1971 issue of the *Washington University Law Quarterly*; permission to utilize this is granted. We wish to acknowledge with gratitude the permission to quote made by the following publishers: Harvard University Press (for quotations from John P. Frank, *Justice Daniel Dissenting* [1964]), and the Washington *Star* (for a quotation from Lyle Dennison's column, "Washington Whirligig").

Contents

Preface

It is the purpose of this book to explore the relationship of the Supreme Court and Congress. Of particular interest is the validity of a widely held academic conception that Congressmen share an attitude of reverence for the Supreme Court which, in times of crisis, serves to protect the Court from serious institutional attacks. The conceptual frame reference of Walter Burnham's emphasis upon time series analysis,[1] and of contemporary investigations of the impact of judicial decisions,[2] is basic to this study. A broader perspective for understanding the nature of Congress–Court relations may be gained by utilization of an investigatory emphasis which embodies a convergence of interest group analysis and roll call behavioral studies in chronological sequence.

The intellectual obligations which the authors accumulated are large and diverse. Challenging teachers at their respective graduate schools, stimulating colleagues at Iowa and Southern California, and helpful and interested colleagues in the House of Representatives contributed immeasurably. Professors Gordon Baker, Dean Mann, and Henry Turner at the University of California, Santa Barbara, were particularly helpful throughout the project, and Gordon K. Zenk provided invaluable assistance with computer programming. Professor Walter Murphy provided an incisive critique of the manuscript. Several graduate assistants, particularly David Engels, Albert Melone, and Don Riley rendered valuable work. Iowa's Political Research Laboratory and its excellent staff were exceedingly helpful. The roll call analysis of Congressional attacks on the Supreme Court, 1945–

1. Walter Dean Burnham, *Critical Elections and the Main Springs of American Politics* (New York: W. W. Norton and Company, Inc., 1970).

2 Stephen L. Wasby, *The Impact of the United States Supreme Court: Some Perspectives* (Homewood, Illinois: The Dorsey Press, 1970).

1968, were supported by the National Science Foundation (Grant GS–2862).

Needless to say, any errors or interpretative responsibilities must be assumed by the authors. In particular, the National Science Foundation and its personnel do not acquire responsibility by osmosis.

John R. Schmidhauser
University of Iowa
Larry L. Berg
University of Southern California

I

Introduction

Modern academic interpretations of the status of the Supreme Court in the American political system have commonly accepted the notion that the Supreme Court is protected from political attack by an aura of reverence. The Court Packing Fight of 1937 was the seminal controversy which allegedly provided the basis for such an assumption. By the 1960s, the "reverence" for the Court idea became a basic explanatory concept in assessments of Congress' relationship to the Supreme Court.

To what extent is Congressional antagonism toward the Court "recent"? Has there been a truly significant change in Congressional attitudes in the last three or four decades? Were the bitter ideological attacks leveled against Fortas because of Congressional antagonism to the thrust of the Warren Court decisions uncharacteristic of Congress–Court relations in the 20th century? Has the shift from a pro-business anti-regulatory position by the Roosevelt, Stone, Vinson, and Warren Courts ultimately eroded significant and influential bases for support in American society?

Truly great contributors to the literature of the legal process have likened the evolution of law and its institutions to the complexity of an ancient tapestry. Holmes once said,

> When I think then of the law, I see a princess mightier than she who once wrought at Bayeux, eternally weaving meaning into such dim figures of the ever lengthening past—figures too dim to be noticed by the idle, too symbolic to be interpreted except by her pupils, but to the discerning eye disclosing every painful step

> and every world-shaking contest by which mankind has worked and fought its way from savage isolation to organic social life.[1]

In the context of contemporary studies of legal institutions, such emphasis upon diversity and complexity often is a prelude to eschewing the use of mathematical or other nontraditional methods, particularly among those prone to deplore the behavioral. In fact, recognition of the infinite variety of human and institutional developments can and, indeed, should be an integral part of modern research on the judicial process. Utilization of behavioral methods of analysis has, at least in recent years, been accepted by most as complementary to the use of conventional methods.[2]

Gerhard Loewenberg, in presenting an analysis of the current status and goals of legislative research before the 1969 Shambaugh Conference on Comparative Legislative Behavior Research,[3] concluded with the admonition that

> In order to pursue fruitful comparative research, we will not only have to engage in conceptual clarification, but to free ourselves from the tyranny of method. . . .
>
> Methodological developments have also bemused us into an insistence that comparative research can only be undertaken if the most sophisticated methods developed in the study of U.S. legislatures are identically applied to the study of their non-American counterparts. . . .

Loewenberg's particular emphases are also relevant to the utilization of particular theoretical approaches such as systems theory. One may indeed object to the implied acceptance of a mechanical analogy; perhaps the conception of human behavior and institutional development implicit in the world view of those motivated by the compelling optimistic spirit of the Renaissance—whether a da Vinci or a Jefferson—is more appropriate. Whether accepted as theory or as an interesting approach, the attempt to view a political system as a totality recognizes not only the interrelationship of institutional

[1] Reproduced at the Law School of the University of California, Berkeley, California.

[2] See Alan F. Westin's review of Glendon R. Schubert, *The Judicial Mind: Attitudes and Ideologies of Supreme Court Justices, 1946–1963* and *Judicial Behavior: A Reader in Theory and Judicial Behavior* in *61 American Political Science Review* (September, 1967), pp. 763–764.

[3] Gerhard Loewenberg, "Toward a Paradigm for Legislative Research," *Shambaugh Conference on Comparative Legislative Research* (Iowa City, Iowa, May 26–30, 1969).

roles but also the concept of simultaneity, at least implicitly. In essence, the processes of government operate simultaneously. Although the spontaneity implicit in such processes is difficult to replicate in social science research, it is important to recognize this dimension. The omission or relative lack of interest in legislative-judicial interrelations in most of the literature on legislative behavior stands in stark contrast to the proliferation of writing and research on executive-legislative relations. As the discussion in Chapter 3 indicates, such unexamined influences can seriously distort the anticipated conceptions of the governmental process in a given political system. The conceptual framework of systems theory can help to meet this problem.

Utilizing the basic conceptual framework of systems theory, we will attempt to determine the essential nature of Court-Congress relationships from the perspective of the overall political system. These relationships are not static but rather ever-changing. Thus, the responsibilities are often blurred, tenuous, and prone to conflict as each system attempts to carry out its responsibilities in making authoritative social decisions which have impact both on the political system and on the social system of which it is a part. As Keefe and Ogul have stated, "... functioning in related but poorly defined spheres, legislators and courts inevitably clash at critical intersections of the political process."[4]

We will broaden the traditional approach, which has placed great emphasis upon analysis of Supreme Court decisions and the formal responses, if any, of the Congress to these decisions. However, in order to discover the salient characteristics of the relationship of Congress and the Supreme Court it is necessary also to examine the impact on the Court of legislative action or inaction in vital policy areas of the political system. Recent history suggests that legislative inaction is an important determinant of input demands on the Court (as, for example, in reapportionment and civil rights questions).

The second and closely related objective of this study will be to examine the institutional influences which may, through historical development, divide and distinguish the approaches to national problems by Congress and by the Supreme Court. Professor Ralph Huitt, formerly assistant secretary for legislation in the Department

[4] William J. Keefe and Morris S. Ogul, *The American Legislative Process: Congress and the States* (Englewood Cliffs, New Jersey: Prentice-Hall, Inc., 1968), p. 454.

of Health, Education, and Welfare, provided a compelling rationale for examining institutional influences in his introductory chapter in *Lawmakers in a Changing World.* Although he emphasizes the tensions inherent in the relationship of Congress and the career bureaucracy, Huitt's approach has particular relevance to the study of Congressional–judicial relationships. This approach is summed up by his observation that "Men who spend much or most of their adult lives in a social system as highly institutionalized as Congress and the bureaucracy, where careers are long and status and influence depend so much on tenure, are profoundly shaped in their attitudes by the institution itself.[5]

It should be noted that the phrase "judicial behavior" has, because of contemporary emphasis upon techniques such as Guttman scaling and mathematical and arithmetical box scores, usually connoted the making of judicial decisions. Although decision-making is indeed an integral component of the analysis of Congress–Supreme Court relationships, focussing attention on institutional roles necessitates also utilizing an older and broader conception of institutional behavior, one which embraces every step in the life-cycle of judges and legislators. We feel that this broader approach will render more understandable the respective roles these men play in the American political system and that it will result in a more coherent interpretation of the ever-changing relationship of Congress and the Supreme Court.

[5] Ralph K. Huitt, "Congress, the Durable Partner" in Elke Frank (ed.), *Lawmakers in a Changing World* (Englewood Cliffs, New Jersey: Prentice-Hall, Inc., 1966), p. 12.

2

The Congress and the Court: Myths and Realities

January, 1965, marked the opening of a Congressional session described by the press corps in superlatives. The "fabulous 89th" compiled a legislative record which elicited the judgment that significant changes had permanently altered the role and structure of the Congress. Professor Stephen K. Bailey concluded that "basic political, economic, and sociological changes in the American society, and in the world at large, have finally forced a series of adjustments in the structure and role of the Congress so profound as to merit the term 'revolution.'"[1] Bailey identified five major events as symbols of these basic changes. It is significant that two were decisions of the Supreme Court: *Brown* v. *Board of Education* and *Wesberry* v. *Sanders*. Bailey posited that *Brown* "symbolized the fact that the national legislature could no longer serve as a terminal barrier to the achievement of equal rights for Negroes," while *Wesberry* "helped loosen the stranglehold of rural conservatism on the House of Representatives."[2] The other three symbols of change were (a) the enlargement of the House Rules Committee in 1961, (b) the use of cloture to effect Senate passage of civil rights legislation in 1964 and voting rights legislation in 1965, and (c) the passage of the Internal Revenue Act of 1964, embodying an alleged Congressional

[1] Stephen K. Bailey, *The New Congress* (New York: St. Martin's Press, 1966), p. vii.
[2] *Ibid.*

acceptance of the "New Economics." For the more optimistic, the adoption of major procedural reforms at the opening of the 89th Congress, notably the "21-day rule," served to buttress Bailey's hypothesis.

Scarcely a year after Professor Bailey's analysis, veteran newsman Jack Anderson summed up the return to "normalcy" when he commented that the 90th Congress "is run by a gaggle of old men from small towns. . . . Congress has become largely a council of elders, dominated by tired old men whose only claim to power is their ability to outlive their colleagues."[3]

The judgment that Congress had reverted to conventional obstructionism was accompanied in 1967 by a full-scale resumption of frontal attacks on the Supreme court. Holmes Alexander's column entitled "The Nine-Man Terror Squad" was typical of the new mood:

> Some countries fear their military or their secret police—but America '67 fears its Supreme Court.
>
> How can you tell what that black-robed elite are going to do next? Spring more criminals? Abolish more protections? Throw down more altars? Rewrite more laws? Chew more clauses out of the Constitution? Maybe, as a former Vice President once said, the American people are too dumb to understand, but I wouldn't bet on that. I would bet that the outcropping of evidence at the top—in testimony before the U.S. Senate—says something about a swelling concern among the people themselves.[4]

The true test of institutional change is not, of course, to be found only in the press. But the tone and temper of contemporary political discourse is often reflected therein. The contrast between Bailey's and Alexander's views may be dismissed as typical of the divergence between the classroom and the pressroom. Yet the difference highlights the fundamental question of what the institutional relationship of Congress and the Court "normally" is.

WHAT IS THE "NORMAL" CONGRESSIONAL–COURT RELATIONSHIP?

Of particular importance to the study of the Congress–Supreme Court relationship is the question of whether a remarkable fluctua-

[3] *Cedar Rapids Gazette*, August 7, 1967, p. 6.

[4] Holmes Alexander, "The Nine-Man Terror Squad," *Keokuk Gate City*, July 24, 1967, p. 12.

tion did indeed take place in so short a span of time. The first matter to be explored is the question, "What is the 'normal' relationship of the Congress to the Supreme Court?" The focus of attention is the post-World-War-II era. The excellent works of C. Herman Pritchett and Walter Murphy were of particular importance to us in delineating the issues of this modern period.[5]

Throughout much of the postwar era, the relationship of the Congress and the Supreme Court was characteristically marked by political attrition, highlighted by crises of potentially great seriousness. The frontal attacks upon the Supreme Court in the aftermath of the urban riots suggest that 1967 marked the beginning of another significant period of accentuated conflict between legislature and court. The incisive studies by Pritchett and Murphy, footnoted above, have emphasized the ideological basis for the legislative-judicial conflicts of the period after World War II. Both studies distinguished carefully the various forms of interaction between Congress and the Supreme Court. Historically, Congress has been importuned from time to time to weaken or completely blunt the impact of judicial decisions. Special interest groups have often taken such action in the name of some imposing constitutional principle such as states rights. Congressional resolution of the Tidelands Oil controversy represents a classic modern example of the use of statutory change to effectuate special-interest goals. Such statutory revision of judicial interpretation is commonplace in modern times.

A second characteristic of the relationship of Congress and the Court in the postwar era has been Congressmen's repeated use of the Court as a rhetorical target in ideological controversies. Although the tactic is by no means unique to the modern era, a distinct change, in fact, has occurred. "Scapegoating" has become commonplace, as members of Congress are generally aware that the justices cannot "fight back." Indeed, such use of the Court has become so firm a part of Congressional behavior that it survives contemporary ideological and political changes in the composition of the Congress. This

[5] See, for example, C. Herman Pritchett, *The Roosevelt Court: A Study in Judicial Politics and Values, 1937–1947* (New York: Macmillan Co., 1948); *The Civil Liberties and the Vinson Court* (Chicago: University of Chicago Press, 1953); *The Political Offender and the Warren Court* (Boston: Boston University Press, 1958); *Congress versus the Supreme Court, 1957–1960* (Minneapolis: University of Minnesota (1961); and Walter F. Murphy, *Congress and the Court* (Chicago: University of Chicago Press, 1962).

development contrasts sharply with the conceptions of Congressional attitudes accepted in the literature of the Court.[6]

The unique and perceptive analysis of Congress and the Constitution by Professor Donald Morgan provided additional insight into the nature of the fundamental changes that have developed in our system. Morgan's study emphasized characteristics of the Congressional process that could contribute to understanding how constitutional issues were treated. Choosing constitutional questions of major importance in different historical periods, Morgan examined three factors: the characteristics of the participants in each settlement, their attitudes and ideology concerning the constitutional role, and the mode of settlement.[7] Morgan contended that many studies of Congress had overemphasized the factor of interest-group conflict and minimized the significance of deliberation.[8]

Morgan's emphasis upon legislative deliberation and Pritchett's and Murphy's perceptive studies of ideological differences between Congress and the Court may be supplemented by additional analyses of institutional variations in legislative and judicial treatment of significant public issues and of issues pertaining to the relationship between the executive, legislative, and judicial branches of the national government. Illustrative of the latter was the treatment of the issue of the salary of members of the Supreme Court in the 88th and 89th Congresses. The Congressional debates and roll calls on the salary issue indicate that the modern relationship of the Court to the Congress may well include more fundamental bases for division than transitory ideological differences or changes in the mode of legislative deliberation.

THE JUDICIAL SALARY ISSUE

In the second session of the 88th Congress in 1964, the House and Senate passed the Government Employees Salary Reform Act. The annual salary of members of Congress and of federal judges, *excepting Supreme Court justices*, was increased by $7,500. The justices were granted an increase of $4,500. The $3,000 differential clearly

[6] See the discussion of these conceptions in Chapters 6 and 7.

[7] Donald S. Morgan, *Congress and the Constitution* (Cambridge, Massachusetts: Howard University Press, 1966), pp. 34–36.

[8] *Ibid.*, pp. 13–14.

reflected a direct Congressional reprimand to the Supreme Court. This crude rebuff clearly stemmed from Congressional dissatisfaction with several controversial decisions rendered by the Court. The *American Bar Association Journal* took note of this serious breach in Congress–Court relations in a strong editorial:

> The reason for this discriminatory provision seems inescapably an effort on the part of Congress to punish the members of our highest Court for performing their constitutional duty of deciding cases as they see them. If indeed this was the purpose, it was unworthy of the principle of the division of powers of our government. But even worse it is an affront to the principle of the independence of the judiciary.

The editorial concluded with a strong request to Congress "to correct the flagrant injustice done to the nine men who hold the highest and most solemn responsibility of the administration of justice."[9]

Judicial Salaries and the 89th Congress

The results of the 1964 election indicated, according to many news media accounts, a sweeping change not only in membership in the House and Senate but in the basic ideology of the majorities in each house.

The House of Representatives was called to order by the Clerk of the House, Ralph R. Roberts, on January 4, 1965. Thus began the 1st session of the 89th Congress. The Chaplain, Rev. Bernard Braskamp, echoed the chorus of press-corps optimism when he asked newly elected and veterans alike to "give our Republic and our democracy a new image, one that is more righteous and radiant, more meaningful and magnanimous."[10] Reverend Braskamp's prayer seemed to augur well for the justices of the Supreme Court. Since the hostile closing weeks of the 88th Congress, many new members had replaced members of the "conservative coalition." "Judge" Howard Smith, chairman of the House Rules Committee, was stripped of his power to pigeonhole progressive legislation when the House adopted a procedural reform called the "21-day rule" on the first day of the 89th Congress. A wide range of legislative

[9] *50 American Bar Association Journal,* p. 1151 (1964).
[10] *Congressional Record,* January 4, 1965, p. 14.

programs concerned with domestic problems moved speedily toward adoption. Early in the session a bill, H.R. 5374, to increase the salaries of Supreme Court justices was introduced, in order to restore the previous salary differential between the justices and other federal judges. Speedy correction seemed imminent when the House Judiciary Committee reported the bill without dissent.[11] However, when the bill was considered by the House of Representatives on March 17, 1965, it encountered a carefully organized attack.

Immediately after presentation of House Resolution 276 embodying the rules governing the handling of the salary bill, Congressman H. R. Gross made the point of order that a quorum was not present. Four hundred and one members responded. In the debate on the adoption of a rule permitting discussion of H.R. 5374, the opposition used their time primarily to voice criticisms of recent Supreme Court decisions. Although Congressman Gross of Iowa opened the attack with the jurisdictional question of committee sponsorship,[12] the major frontal attack on the Court was mounted early in the discussion by Congressman (now Senator) Bob Dole of Kansas.

Dole immediately suggested that the Congress in effect blackmail the Court into acceptance of a policy of reversal of its recently adopted "one-man-one-vote" decision. In his opening statement Dole remarked pointedly that

> I take this time because whenever thinking of the Supreme Court I think of last June 15, 1964, and reapportionment decisions handed down in *Reynolds against Simms* and the related cases. It has been suggested that perhaps section 2 of the bill might be amended whereby the effective date of the pay increase if adopted by this House, would be the date the Supreme Court reverses the decision in *Reynolds against Simms.*[13]

Dole later conceded that such an amendment was not germane but persisted in relating his opposition to salary adjustment to what was currently a strong drive by the American Farm Bureau Federation to

[11] H.R. Rep. No. 136, 89th Congress, 1st session (1965).

[12] Gross argued that the bill should have been handled by the House Post Office and Civil Service Committee (of which he was a member) rather than the Judiciary Committee. This argument was obviously diversionary and was factually rebutted by Judiciary Committee Chairman Emmanuel Celler of New York. *Congressional Record*, March 17, 1965, p. 5126.

[13] *Ibid.*

secure signatures on a discharge petition aimed at freeing from committee a bill reversing the *Reynolds* v. *Simms* decision.

Other opponents of the Court such as Wayne Hays of Ohio, Paul Jones of Missouri, and Joe Waggoner of Louisiana attacked what they termed judicial assumption of legislative power. As Jones put it, if the justices "are going to assume the legislative functions of Government, let them be paid on that basis." When Jones was reminded that there was a Constitutional prohibition against reduction of current judges' salaries, he retorted, "They do not pay any attention to the Constitution any more anyhow."[14] This unenlightening and often irrelevant debate terminated in a demand for a vote on the rule. Although the rule was adopted, the margin of 202 to 183 was a harbinger of difficulties to come in full House consideration of the corrective measure.

Chairman Emmanuel Celler led support for the bill in the Committee of the Whole. Celler's comment that "I did not know when the bill was brought up that we would have had a sort of field day of criticism against our highest court" was a candid admission that the strong attack on the Court had caught committee and House leadership by surprise. Celler and a number of other supporters of the salary bill then not only presented a factual defense of the proposal but also declared that the attacks on the Court made the vote a test of the "integrity and independence of the Court." Another supporter, Corman of California, provided a detailed historical summary of the relationship among Congressional, Presidential, and judicial salaries, indicating that relative salary equivalence had long been accepted.

Although supporters of the bill endeavored to maintain a temperate, factual tone, the opposition returned to a frontal assault on the Court and, in fact, resorted to personal attacks on individual members of the Court. Justice Douglas was the favorite target. For example, when the topic of widows' annuities was discussed, John Bell Williams of Mississippi asked, "While you are on the subject of the judges' widows, I would like to know when Justice Douglas passes on how many of his widows we will be required to compensate?" Celler expressed the hope that "sober judgment will descend upon him and he will strike those remarks from the record." Williams needless to say, did not strike his remarks. Rather, he was

[14] *Ibid.*

gleefully joined by Gross, who commented on Justice Douglas' mountain climbing. Although several members rose to argue that their opposition was not based on disagreement with the Court's decisions, Paul Jones' summation of the opposition's arguments had wide support. Jones once again contended that the Supreme Court "has gone beyond its duties."[15] A vote against the salary adjustment was equated with opposition to the Court, its members, and its decisions. The roll call mustered 177 House members for the bill, 203 against, and 53 absentions. The defeat of the justices' salary adjustment bill stirred little public discussion.

The legislative history of the justices' salary issue as treated in the House of Representatives was not presented here for purely descriptive purposes. Other legislative actions expressive of fundamental public policy and ideological conflicts with the Supreme Court were taken during the sessions of the 89th Congress, but the House consideration of the justices' salary adjustment provided a unique situation for a discussion of the role of the Court in the modern era, with freedom from complex technical arguments. Although a few members argued otherwise, the issue was clearly whether the House would reprimand the Court or not. In contrast to the situation in the late 1950s when anti-Court legislation such as the *Jenner-Butler* bill and H.R. 3 attracted widespread support, including some elements of the legal profession,[16] the salary bill had the support of most elements of the bar and of the full House Judiciary Committee prior to floor action.

What factors in addition to the element of surprise contributed to the defeat? It is here that Huitt's emphasis upon institutional analysis is particularly important, because the ordinary explanations simply do not suffice. The monumental indifference to the basic Constitutional issue that was the outstanding characteristic of the House debate reflected more than transitory ideological conflict and the ever-present temptation to "politic" on the floor for the folks back home. Only a handful of members, mostly old-timers like Celler, demonstrated a grasp of the historic and Constitutional implications of the debate. Indeed Celler's appeal in that debate to the lessons of Roosevelt's Court-packing plan produced an additional bit of evidence of indifference to basic Constitutional issues. One of Celler's new Judiciary Committee members in the 89th Congress proudly

[15] *Ibid.*, pp. H5134–5135.
[16] Morgan, *op. cit.*, pp. 269–291.

dusted off the old Court-packing bill and introduced it in the opening days of the 90th Congress.

Pertinent to this inquiry is the question of whether the legislative response to the salary issue was unique or typical. A considerable body of academic and political literature attests to the alleged reverence in which members of Congress hold the United States Supreme Court. The fate of President Franklin Roosevelt's so-called Court-packing plan is usually cited as striking evidence of this position. But what are the widely accepted academic opinions about the nature of Congressional-Supreme Court relations? Do these opinions find support among members of the Court or members of Congress?

Perhaps the most striking characteristic of Congress-Supreme Court relations in the 20th century is the number of diametrically opposed viewpoints which purport to accurately describe those relations. In 1961, for example, it was argued that "Courts are protected by their magic; only rarely can a hand be laid on a judge without a public outcry of sacrilege."[17] Commenting about the fate of Supreme-Court-curbing legislation in the period 1957–1961, Herman Pritchett suggested that "Basically, the Court was protected by the respect which is so widely felt for the judicial institution in the United States."[18] Glendon Schubert stressed the influence of legal professionalism as a bulwark of the Court in the case of Congressional reversal of statutory interpretation decisions of the Supreme Court: "Many congressmen are lawyers; and the argument that proponents of an amendatory bill are showing disrespect for the highest court in the land is an effective one."[19]

Walter Murphy and Joseph Tanenhaus have provided a preliminary report of their highly sophisticated study of public opinion and the Supreme Court. Their preliminary mapping report indicates, tentatively, that the Supreme Court as an institution is accorded diffuse support which, as the authors describe it, "dips far beneath the Court's attentive public into the more articulate layers of the less

[17] Walter F. Murphy and C. Herman Pritchett, *Courts, Judges and Politics: An Introduction to the Judicial Process* (New York: Random House, 1961), pp. 554–555.

[18] C. Herman Pritchett, *Congress versus the Supreme Court, 1957–1961* (Minneapolis: University of Minnesota Press, 1961), p. 119.

[19] Glendon A. Schubert, *Constitutional Politics: The Political Behavior of Supreme Court Justices and the Constitutional Policies They Make* (New York: Holt, Rinehart and Winston, 1960), pp. 257–258.

knowledgeable."[20] To what extent, if at all, this general public attitude is recognized and deemed significant by members of Congress is not clear. Content analysis of floor debates in the Senate and House of Representatives for two Congresses (1957–1961) led Harry Stumpf to conclude that arguments for the sacrosanct nature of the Supreme Court were seldom raised (and when raised were not persuasive) in opposition to legislation designed to reverse statutory interpretations by the Supreme Court. Stumpf did argue, on the basis of relatively few legislative confrontations, that judicial symbolism was efficacious when invoked against legislation or proposed constitutional amendments designed to weaken the Supreme Court as an institution rather than to reverse ordinary policy positions.[21] Stumpf's content analysis of floor debate provided several interesting exploratory suggestions but offered few clues to the nature of the day-to-day working relationship of the Court and the Congress.

Charles Warren noted, many years ago, that despite the fulsome praise bestowed upon the Supreme Court by its Congressional protagonists in the formative years, the Court was relegated to a basement room in the Capitol for the conduct of its important functions. The vivid description he quoted from a New York newspaper correspondent who had come to Washington to cover the oral argument in *Gibbons* v. *Ogden* does not suggest that the needs of the justices were uppermost in the minds of members of Congress in 1824:

> The apartment is not in a style which comports with the dignity of that body, or which bears a comparison with the other Halls of the Capitol. In the first place, it is like going down cellar to reach it. The room is on the basement story in an obscure part of the north wing. In arriving at it, you pass a labyrinth, and almost need the clue of Ariadne to guide you to the sanctuary of the blind goddess. A stranger might traverse the dark avenues of the Capitol for a week, without finding the remote corner in which Justice is administered to the American Republic . . . a room which is hardly capacious enough for a ward justice. . . .[22]

[20] Walter F. Murphy and Joseph Tanenhaus, "Public Opinion and the United States Supreme Court: Mapping of some Prerequisites for Court Legitimation of Regime Changes," *II Law and Society Review* (May 1968), p. 373.

[21] Harry P. Stumpf, "Congressional Response to Supreme Court Rulings: The Interaction of Law and Politics," *Journal of Public Law* (November 2, 1965), pp. 392–395; and Harry P. Stumpf, "The Political Efficacy of Judicial Symbolism," *19 Western Political Quarterly* (June, 1966), pp. 293–303.

[22] Charles Warren, *The Supreme Court in United States History* (Volume I) (Boston: Little, Brown and Company, 1922), pp. 460–461.

Warren's perceptive citation suggests, implicitly, a cautious comparison of Congressional words and deeds. While modern Congresses finally provided the justices with a new building, dubbed the "Marble Palace" by John Frank,[23] there remain areas of considerable misunderstanding and institutional tension over Congress' budgetary and housekeeping roles.

THE BUDGET FOR JUDICIAL ADMINISTRATION: SHALL CONGRESS BE HELD IN CONTEMPT?

From the perspective of Congress, the justices and judges of the federal judiciary are sometimes viewed as rather cavalier in the treatment of their statutory responsibilities. In a report to the Senate Appropriations Committee submitted in 1959, Paul Cotter presented a field study of the operations of the federal courts that pinpointed several areas of Congressional criticism.[24] The Judicial Conference of the United States under the supervision of the Chief Justice and the circuit judicial councils and conferences were described by Cotter as "the judiciary's system of self-government." In reporting to the Senate Appropriations committee, Cotter criticized the judicial administrative performance severely, charging that it had been "torturously slow and inadequate in bringing about reforms and improvements. . . ." Citing "a very serious lack of administrative control and direction throughout the whole system," Cotter charged the judges and justices with failure to fulfill specific duties under law. In Cotter's words,

> The most startling and paradoxical condition found, however, was the general disregard of a 20-year-old law which charges the judicial council of each circuit with the supervision of district court dockets; requires the Administrative Office of the United States Courts to submit to these councils quarterly reports based on examination of the district court dockets; and requires the judicial council of each circuit to take such action thereon as is

[23] For a discussion of historic changes in the work and social habits of the justices see John P. Frank, *Marble Palace: The Supreme Court in American Life* (New York: Alfred A. Knopf, 1958), pp. 107–129.

[24] Paul Cotter, "Field Study of the Operations of the United States Courts," *Report to the Senate Appropriations Committee* (Washington, D.C., Committee Print, 1959), pp. 1–5, 16–29.

> necessary, and to make all necessary orders for the effective and expeditious administration of the business of the courts within its circuit.

Congressional sensitivity toward the uneven administrative performance of the federal judiciary is reciprocated by the judiciary. Indeed, the tensions between the judicial and legislative branches over budgetary and housekeeping issues have apparently mounted in recent years. Thus on March 15, 1969, Chief Justice Earl Warren broke tradition and publicly criticized Congress for its neglect of the federal judiciary in strong and direct terms.[25] Addressing the Bar Association of the District of Columbia, the Chief Justice stated bluntly that "it is next to impossible for the courts to get something from Congress." He stressed that the increasing crime problem is attributable "to the fact that we do not move along to get cases tried." In order to "keep cases current we must get a response from Congress to do our job in a proper way." Warren then emphasized pointedly: "Do you think we can get any help from Congress? The answer has clearly been no."

The Chief Justice then enumerated several instances in which Congress ignored modest requests to assist the Court in meeting an increasingly heavier workload. He stated, "One time I asked for a messenger for the library. This was at a time when the Congress was building the great Rayburn Building. But the request for the messenger was striken from the appropriation."

"In the last three years," the Chief Justice continued, "because the number of cases have increased so much, we wanted to add one law clerk for each justice. You would think (from the Congressional reaction) that we were just dipping our hands into the Treasury." Although the caseload of the Supreme Court had more than doubled since Warren became Chief Justice, the full request for clerks was not met by Congress after 16 years.

Warren described Congressional expenditures for the judiciary as "just a drop in the bucket. . . . the F.B.I. budget is infinitely higher than the whole Federal Court system." In fiscal 1969, according to the *Washington Post*, Congress authorized \$220 million for the F.B.I. and \$102.4 million for the entire federal judiciary. The Chief Justice underscored that "other branches of government proliferate without

[25] Chief Justice Earl Warren, address to the Bar Association of the District of Columbia, *Washington Post*, March 16, 1969, pp. A1, A4.

end. But not the courts. . . . We can't go over and lobby and we can't trade anything with the committees."

Warren concluded his talk with a portrayal of the consequences of Congressional penny-pinching for the poor. He asserted that "Congress just hasn't kept up with the needs of the court system." The result has been a huge criminal-trial backlog. Commenting that the average time interval between indictment and jury trial in the federal court for New York (Brooklyn) was over 20 months, Chief Justice Warren stated "It's going on all over the country." Speaking of this kind of delay, the retiring Chief Justice summed up: "Just think of what that means to a criminal defendant who is innocent. He is either under a cloud and must suffer the shame of his neighbors, or he is in jail. And a guilty man on bail can go out and commit other crimes."

Warren's criticism of Congress brought into the arena of public discussion a very important aspect of the institutional relationship of Congress and the Supreme Court. With respect to the institutional norms of the Court itself, Warren, during his tenure as Chief Justice, had not only avoided direct criticism but had refrained from giving addresses to local bar associations. His address to the District of Columbia Bar was the first he had made since becoming Chief Justice. Warren indicated that he originally accepted the local bar association invitation when he anticipated an earlier retirement.

Warren's critique, while unusual as a public attack on Congress by a Chief Justice, was, in substance, similar to several recent criticisms voiced by inferior federal judges. For example, when Warren E. Burger was a member of the U.S. Court of Appeals for the District of Columbia, he leveled a very specific public criticism at Congress in an address to the Young Lawyers Section of the District of Columbia Bar Association on October 31, 1967.[26] Burger pointed out that the additional judicial administrative work created by passage of the Bail Reform and Criminal Justice Acts had fallen upon already overburdened clerks, marshals, and other employees of the General Sessions and District Courts. The Criminal Justice Act provided for government-paid fees for attorneys for indigent defendants, and the Bail Reform Act allowed almost all defendants charged with noncapital crimes to be freed on pretrial release. Inability to post a monetary bond was eliminated as a condition that

[26] Appeals Court Judge Warren E. Burger succeeded Earl Warren as Chief Justice.

would keep a defendant in jail. Commenting on these recent statutory developments, Judge Burger indicated that

> Congress, having sole power of the purse, failed to provide adequate staffs to administer either of these two statutes and that failure has been disastrous.
>
> A coordinator was needed to administer the selection, appointment and the processing of the system and fixing compensation of the hundreds of lawyers involved under the Criminal Justice Act. Congress provided for none.
>
> In addition, a substantial staff including investigators was needed to administer the Bail Reform Act, but Congress gave only \$75,000—which meets only a fraction of the need.[27]

As had Warren, Burger concluded by enumerating the serious consequences of Congressional parsimony. While court personnel, both judges and supporting staff, had not increased significantly in the past 18 years, the criminal case load in the federal courts of the District of Columbia had increased by 40%. The median time between indictment and final disposition in trial court had risen from 39 days in 1950 to 60 days in 1960 and 116 days in 1967.

Congress' budgetary responses or nonresponses to the Supreme Court and the inferior federal judiciary deserve special emphasis because they are an often neglected but nevertheless highly significant aspect of Congress-Court day-to-day relations. Most importantly, budgetary relations may, as indicated by Chief Justice Warren and his successor, be intimately related to the ability of the federal judiciary to perform its functions efficiently and effectively.

[27] Judge Warren E. Burger, address to the Young Lawyers Section of the District of Columbia Bar Association, *Washington Post*, November 1, 1969, p. C10.

3

Legitimacy and Judicial Power

The supports essential to institutional stability and effectiveness are conceptualized appropriately in the terms *consensus* and *legitimacy*. Goldman and Jahnige argue that one of the conditions for "a positive flow of supports" is that "the courts must operate in a judicial manner." Recognizing that some of the demands "fed into the federal judicial system are not greatly different from those fed into other institutions," the authors nevertheless concluded that judicial processing of demands is substantially different from bureaucratic and legislative processing.[1] Indeed, this view of the relationship between institutional tradition and public and/or professional support was basic to the personal philosophy of the late Justice Felix Frankfurter. His comments in *Public Utilities Commission* v. *Pollack*[2] represent a classic expression of this viewpoint. Frankfurter stated that:

> The judicial process demands that a judge move within the framework of relevant legal rules and the covenanted modes of thought for ascertaining them. He must think dispassionately and submerge private feeling on every aspect of a case. There is a good deal of shallow talk that the judicial robe does not change the man within it. It does. The fact is that on the whole judges do lay aside private views in discharging their judicial functions. This is achieved through training, professional habits, self-discipline and

[1] Sheldon Goldman and Thomas P. Jahnige, *The Federal Judicial System: Readings in Process and Behavior* (New York: Holt, Rinehart and Winston, 1968) p. 76.

[2] 343 U.S. 466–467 (1959).

that fortunate alchemy by which men are loyal to the obligation with which they are entrusted. But it is also true that reason cannot control the subconscious influence of feelings of which it is unaware. When there is ground for believing that such unconscious feelings may operate in the ultimate judgment, or may not unfairly lead others to believe they are operating, judges recuse themselves. They do not sit in judgment. They do this for a variety of reasons. The guiding consideration is that the administration of justice should reasonably appear to be disinterested as well as be so in fact.

This case for me presents such a situation. My feelings are so strongly engaged as a victim of the practice in controversy that I had better not participate in judicial judgment upon it. I am explicit as to the reason for my non-participation in this case because I have from some time been of the view that it is desirable to state why one takes himself out of a case.

Frankfurter's statement may give compelling support to those academicians who have argued that such factors as regionalism or party affiliation are generally weakened by the countervailing influence of institutional factors. Professor Karl Llewellyn has further described the tradition of the higher appellate courts as follows:[3]

> . . . in the craft-tradition of the appellate courts, we find a number of attributes . . . which are seldom phrased. . . . (These are) effort at "impartiality"; effort to keep the mind open till both sides have been heard; effort to dissociate the "true essence" of the controversy from accidents of person, personality or the like; avoidance of a case in which a judge is or may be thought personally interested . . . .
>
> . . . Some portion of this is institutionalized. "Independence of the judiciary" . . . and non-reducibility of salary, seek both to make much "judicial conduct possible and to further it." Rules of law against bribery, practices set against "influence," loose but useful practices of self-disqualification, even looser but still recognizable practices about judicial manners, the disciplinary pressure of phrasing an explanation of a decision in a published opinion, the policing power of possible open dissent by any member of the court who may see or feel outrage—these form a gap-filled hedge to mark and to half-police the tradition.

[3] Karl N. Llewellyn, "American Common Law Tradition and American Democracy," *1 Journal of Legal and Political Sociology* (1942), p. 32.

Yet Llewellyn recognized, as have candid members of the Supreme Court, that the very institutional traditions which provided a basis for judicial aloofness from contemporary political battles also provided an opportunity for judicial involvement through diligent search for policy alternatives. Thus, in the 20th-century controversy over *stare decisis*, Llewellyn was once moved to observe that "the doctrine of precedent is two-headed . . . Janus-faced. . . . There is one doctrine for getting rid of precedents deemed troublesome and one doctrine for making use of precedents that seem helpful."[4] Similarly, Justice Louis Brandeis stressed that "movement in constitutional interpretation and application—often involving no less striking departures from doctrines previously established—takes place also without specific overruling or qualification of earlier cases."[5] The ambivalence over the Court's institutional role is, of course, not limited to interpretations of institutional procedure and custom. It has been an essential characteristic of the larger role associated with the Supreme Court in its relationship to the broad constitutional principles of federalism and separation of powers. This studied ambivalence was aptly described by Robert Dahl when he commented that "as a political institution, the Court is highly unusual, not least because Americans are not quite willing to accept the fact that it *is* a political institution and not quite capable of denying it; so that frequently we take both positions at once."[6]

These matters obviously have a bearing upon the nature of the supports buttressing the Supreme Court. One crucial dimension relates to the traditional basis for the legitimacy of the Supreme Court's role in the American political system.[7] What was expected of the Supreme Court by its political architects, the designers of the Constitution of 1787? In terms of institutional modes of operation, was there a sharp distinction between the "political" branches of the federal government and the judicial in the formative years? Is there a

[4] Karl N. Llewellyn, *The Bramble Bush* (Oceana edition, 1951), pp. 66–69.

[5] See *Burnet* v. *Coronado Oil and Gas Company*, 285 U.S. 393, 408, note 2, for his citation of examples.

[6] Robert A. Dahl, "Decision-Making in a Democracy: The Supreme Court as a National Policy-Maker," *6 Journal of Politics* (1957), p. 279.

[7] It is important to underscore the difference between "legitimacy" and "legitimation" of regime changes. The former term embraces the fundamental question of whether the Supreme Court was granted or properly assumed the power of judicial review and its significant authority as arbiter in federal-state relations. The latter, as Murphy and Tanenhaus indicated, refers to judicial validation of specific public policies. Murphy and Tanenhaus, *op. cit.*, p. 359.

firm historical basis for the sort of institutional diversity presently attributed to the Congress and the Supreme Court?

Interestingly enough, Charles Warren's research suggests that prior to the adoption of the constitution of 1787, a clear-cut distinction between judicial, legislative, and executive functions did not exist either in the governmental institutions of Great Britain or in the variety of colonial governments developed under the aegis of the mother country (or in some instances developed in spite of it!).

The conditions that perpetuated the overlapping of judicial, legislative, and executive functions in the later colonial period varied from colony to colony; but throughout colonial America, several general factors could be found in virtually every governmental setting. In all of the colonies, the legislature initially was the sole court of law. As each colony developed, the colonial governor or his administrative subordinates often assumed many of the judicial responsibilities originally handled by the colonial legislatures. Separate and independent courts did not emerge in many of the colonies until a half century or more after the development of the colony. The presiding judge was usually the only member of the court with any legal training. In turn, presiding judges were generally under the direct influence of the royal governors. The unity of functions often reflected the practices of Great Britain or local adaptations thereof.[8]

On the eve of the Revolution, the practice of unifying judicial with legislative and executive functions became suspect because it was associated with monarchical abuse of the colonies. The Chancellor of South Carolina, Henry W. De Saussure, recalled in 1817 that

> The emigrants brought with them a deep abhorrence of the intolerance and tyranny of those princes [Charles I, Charles II, James II]; and especially of the great abuses prevailing in the courts of justice. And they partook of the general joy in the prodigious securities obtained in the subsequent reigns of civil and political liberty; among which, the establishment of the independence of the judges formed a principal feature. Their attachment to these principles was further increased by the mischiefs resulting from the incautious appointments made by the British government, in many instances, of very inferior men to preside in the courts of justice of the colonies, who did no honour to the mother country, and whose irregularities and improper conduct contributed in a

[8] Charles Warren, *A History of the American Bar* (Boston: Little, Brown, and Company, 1913), pp. 1–18.

considerable degree to weaken the attachment of the colonies to the government of Great Britain.[9]

Thus a general sentiment toward separating the judicial function from the legislative and executive arose out of the circumstances leading to the final break with Great Britain. However, the specific role of the judiciary in the development of a new constitution after the Revolutionary War was not determined so much by a general sentiment for a strict separation of powers as by hard political bargaining.

The institutional conception of a judiciary maintaining a constitutional division of powers between the government of a whole nation and the governments of its parts or regional subdivisions was understood prior to the constitutional convention of 1787. The British Empire had persisted in its insistence upon an essentially unitary relationship with its colonies, but the exigencies of time, distance, and European wars had weakened the concept in practice. As the separate American colonies achieved a greater degree of local autonomy, particularly during and after the French and Indian War, conflicts of policy and authority between Great Britain and the colonies and among the colonies themselves proliferated. A quasi-judicial institution of the British Empire, the Committee on Trade and Plantations of the British Privy Council, ultimately resolved many of these disputes.[10]

The advent of the Revolutionary War shifted the settlement of such disputes from Great Britain to North America. Under the provisions of the Articles of Confederation, judicial settlement of conflicts between the states in two exceedingly controversial areas of policy making was established. First, conflicts over boundaries and other matters were subject, in Article IX, to settlements imposed by the Confederation Congress acting as "The last resort on appeal." But Congress was empowered to authorize the states in dispute to create *ad hoc* panels of "commissioners or judges to constitute a court for hearing and determining the matter in question. . . . The judgment and sentence of the court . . . shall be final and conclusive. . . ." A very serious boundary dispute was settled through

[9] *Ibid.*, pp. 9–10.

[10] John R. Schmidhauser, "States Rights and the Origin of the Supreme Court's Power as arbiter in Federal-State Relations," *IV Wayne Law Review* (Spring, 1958), pp. 101–114.

this approach in 1782.[11] Second, a permanent judicial body, the Court of Appeals in Cases of Capture, was established under the Articles of Confederation to settle conflicts between the Confederation Congress and the separate states or among the states. Privateering authorized by the states flourished, and the court of appeals heard 118 cases before the Confederation was replaced by the new federal Constitution.

These rudimentary experiments with the substitution of a judicial for a legislative institution were part of the contemporary experience that the delegates to the Philadelphia Constitutional Convention drew upon in 1787. Yet it would be an overstatement to assume that there was strong support for a powerful independent judicial branch of government.

The preponderance of historical evidence suggests that creation of a Supreme Court with broad jurisdiction over controversies heretofore settled by political negotiations between the states or between the states and the Confederation Congress was largely the result of a series of compromises. The viewpoint of the nationalists in the Philadelphia convention was summed up by James Madison years after the issue was settled. He pointed out that "... the obvious necessity of a control on the laws of the states so far as they might violate the constitution and laws of the United States left no option, but as to mode...." The alternatives were "a veto [executive] on the passage of the state laws, a congressional repeal of them, a judicial annulment of them." The issue of federalism had a far greater bearing upon the creation of a Supreme Court than did the concept of separation of powers, although the latter was discussed, albeit inconclusively, during the convention.

The nationalists in the Philadelphia convention originally preferred an executive or legislative veto over the states; conversely their opponents urged that such power be vested in what they considered a weaker and more impartial agency, the Supreme Court incorporated in the Paterson Plan. Ultimately, the Supreme Court was created only after a rather complex series of developments. Chief among these were (a) the repudiation of the principle of coercion of states by federal armed force and substitution of coercion of individuals by federal law, (b) the willingness of every major bloc in the connection to establish a federal judiciary of some kind, (c) the

[11] Merrill Jensen, *The New Nation: A History of the United States during the Confederation, 1781–1789* (New York: Alfred Knopf, Inc., 1951), pp. 335–337.

insistent demand of one major group, the nationalists, for creation of a complete system of inferior federal courts, (d) the defeat of executive and legislative veto power over anti-federal actions of the states and the substitution by Luther Martin of a supremacy clause, and (e) the general tendency to view a federal judiciary as a potential protector of individual and states' rights indicated in the proposals for a Council of Revision.[12]

Strong nationalists were not opposed to creation of a Supreme Court but felt it would not be capable of curbing states' rights and tendencies. As James Wilson put it, in a final appeal for a congressional negative of state laws, "the firmness of judges is not of itself sufficient. Something further is requisite—it will be better to prevent the passage of an improper law, than to declare it void when passed."[13]

Thomas Jefferson did not participate in the Philadelphia convention but did engage in an incisive exchange of letters with James Madison on the relative merits of the congressional negative versus the judicial determination of conflicts in the newly designed federal system. The exchange highlighted the expectations of the nationalists and those who were reluctant to vest too much power in the institutions of the central government. Jefferson, a proponent of the latter, opposed Madison's suggestion for a congressional negative on state laws that conflict with national authority, stating:

> The negative proposed to be given them on all the acts of the several legislatures is now for the first time suggested to my mind. Prima Facie I do not like it. It fails in an essential character, that the hole and the patch be commensurate; but this proposes to mend a small hole by covering the whole garment . . . . Would not an appeal from the state judicatures to a federal court in all cases where the act of confederation controlled the question, be as effectual a remedy, and exactly commensurate to the defect?

After the close of the convention, James Madison addressed himself to that argument, indicating grave doubt that the new judiciary would be able effectively to restrain the states.

> It may be said that the Judicial authority under our new system will keep the states within their proper limits and supply the place of a

[12] For a detailed examination of these developments see Schmidhauser, *op. cit.*, pp. 101–114.

[13] Max Farrand (ed.), *II Records of the Federal Convention* (New Haven: Yale University Press, 1911), pp. 390–391.

> negative on their laws. The answer is that it is more convenient to prevent the passage of a law than to declare it void, after it has passed; that this will be particularly the case where the law aggrieves individuals who may be unable to support an appeal against a State Judiciary, that a state which would violate the legislative rights of the Union would not be very ready to obey a Judicial decree in support of them, and that a recurrence to force, which in the event of disobedience would be a necessity, is an evil which the new Constitution meant to exclude as far as possible. A Constitutional negative on the laws of the states seems equally necessary to secure individuals against encroachments on their rights. The mutability of the laws of the states is found to be a serious evil.[14]

In terms of the concept of supports, it is quite clear that the Supreme Court was, through constitutional fiat, granted an unusual responsibility that by its very nature thrust the judiciary into areas of controversy previously handled by so-called political institutions. In terms of the legitimacy of this broad grant of authority to settle disputes arising out of the nature of the new federalism, the evidence is incontrovertible—the role of the Supreme Court had the support of all major groups in the Philadelphia convention. The discussions that surrounded these developments reflected nationalist concern over the ability of the Court to properly fulfill its obligations, not opposition to the Court's role.

Uncertainty as to the Supreme Court's potential effectiveness provided, ironically, one of the polemical arguments for ratification of the new Constitution. Because a great deal of emphasis has been placed upon power relationships as a crucial factor in the evolution of institutional characteristics, it is interesting to note that one of the major ideological efforts in behalf of the establishment of a Supreme Court was the assurance that such a court would not be a center of countervailing power capable of seriously threatening the legislative and executive branches of government. Alexander Hamilton's famous comment in No. 78 of the Federalist Papers states that

> Whoever attentively considers the different departments of power must perceive, that, in a government in which they are separated from each other, the judiciary, from the nature of its functions, will always be the least dangerous to the political rights of the

[14] Charles Warren, *The Making of the Constitution* (Boston: Little, Brown and Co., 1929), p. 324.

> Constitution; because it will be least in a capacity to annoy or injure them. The Executive not only dispenses the honors, but holds the sword of the community. The legislature not only commands the purse, but prescribes the rules by which the duties and rights of every citizen are to be regulated. The judiciary, on the contrary, has no influence over either the sword or the purse; no direction either of the strength or of the wealth of the society; and can take no active resolution whatever. It may truly be said to have neither Force nor Will, but merely judgment; and must ultimately depend upon the aid of the executive arm even for the efficacy of its judgments.[15]

Hamilton's disclaimer notwithstanding, the nationalists, denominated Federalists, proceeded to enhance the authority of the Supreme Court as soon as the Constitution was ratified. By action of the first Congress, the jurisdiction of the Supreme Court was extended to all cases, state or federal, arising under the Constitution. A system of inferior federal courts was also created over strong opposition by the Anti-Federalists. It may be argued, to be sure, that the action by the first Congress in creating a comprehensive inferior court system was merely an extension of its concern over the necessity for curbing excessive state's rights tendencies. The broad grants of appellate jurisdiction, particularly under Section 25 of this judiciary act, were interpreted largely with this emphasis, although several historians have also argued that the section implied that acts of Congress could be constitutionally reviewed by the Supreme Court as well. Charles Grove Haines pointed out, however, that it was not clear that such a Supreme Court ruling would be final and determinative.[16] In a fundamental sense, the ambivalence modern observers attribute to the Supreme Court in its exercise of constitutional and statutory authority was built into the system by the men who created a new constitution in 1787 and who put it into operation in the first Congress in 1789. Recurring controversies over the distinction between judicial and political matters were destined to become characteristic of Congress–Supreme Court relations in the years after 1789. But the historic record of the origins of the new court unmistakably provides evidence of the legitimacy of broad exercises of authority by the

[15] Alexander Hamilton, in Edward Mead Earle (ed.), *The Federalist* (New York: Random House, 1937), pp. 503–504.

[16] Charles Grove Haines, *The Role of the Supreme Court in American Government and Politics, 1789–1835* (Los Angeles: University of California Press, 1944), pp. 20–24.

Court, even though there was little expectation that the Court's influence in the most controversial of its jurisdictional areas, federalism, would be very strong.

THE EARLY DECADES: THE GROUND RULES ARE ESTABLISHED

In assessing the distinctions between judicial and legislative modes of policy-making, Wells and Grossman emphasized quite appropriately the relative paucity of material on the subject in 1966.[17] Herbert Jacob directly addressed himself to the problem by systematic comparison. He suggested that policy made by judiciaries was narrower in scope than that made by so-called political decision-makers; that the impact of such policies was more often than not applied to governmental institutions rather than the private sectors; that the effects of judicial policy-making were apt to be more uncertain; and that areas of great importance in governmental decision-making, particularly in foreign relations, taxation, and appropriations, were largely outside the scope of judicial decision-making; and finally, that judicial decision-making was by its nature retroactive.[18] Viewed in historic perspective, Jacob's contention that judicial policy-making is narrower in scope is valid on its face because the jurisdiction of the courts is defined by the political branches of government. In some areas judicial authority was purposely circumscribed. However, despite the early historical evidence of serious executive and legislative curtailment of judicial policy-making influence, the federal courts and the Supreme Court in particular possessed the potential to effectively broaden the scope of their policy-making powers as well as to broaden the base of their political support. The controversies of the period from 1789 to 1835 are illustrative.

The provisions of the Constitution gave the Congress discretion over the federal judiciary in a number of crucial areas. The extent of the appellate jurisdiction of the Supreme Court was determined by the Congress in its first session in 1789. Under section 25 of the first judiciary act, state court actions against a claimed federal right were

[17] Richard S. Wells and Joel B. Grossman, "The Concept of Judicial Policy Making," *XV Journal of Public Law* (1966), pp. 286–295, 298–307.

[18] Herbert Jacob, *Justice in America* (Boston: Little, Brown and Co., 1965), pp. 3–33, particularly 30–33.

subject to the jurisdiction of the Supreme Court by writ of error. The first Congress also established an inferior federal court system consisting of district courts and circuit courts. However, there were no circuit judges *per se*. Instead district judges sat with individual members of the Supreme Court as circuit judges. As the circuits expanded with the expansion of the borders of the nation, the circuit duty of the members of the Supreme Court required extensive travel by means of relatively primitive transportation. It also provided rather direct personal contact with the inferior federal jurists and the lesser court officials in every region of the nation. As late as 1959 a president of the American Bar Association recommended restoration of circuit duties for the Supreme Court justices because, he contended, it would keep them in touch with the people.[19] John Randall's recommendation was one of numerous suggestions based on the explicit assumption that there is some sort of relationship between the mode of operation of the Supreme Court and the ideological tendency of its decisions. It is interesting to note that many policy-makers shared the same belief and, consequently, were determined to relate institutional design to desirable ideological goals. Whether the assumption was valid or not, it was frequently acted upon, as emerged clearly in the Congressional and Presidential actions related to the federal judiciary in the early developmental decades of the Supreme Court.

In the initial action establishing an inferior federal judiciary, Senators Oliver Ellsworth and William Paterson (later Chief Justice and Associate Justice, respectively) first pushed for a complete network of inferior federal courts, but they later settled for the more limited version adopted in 1789. By selecting the narrower option, the first Congress clearly made a decided impact upon the style of living of the justices of the Supreme Court. Indeed, during a good many decades, Congress' manipulation of the size and geographic location of the circuits served as a barometer of its approval or disapproval of the Supreme Court's decisions.[20]

Perhaps the most striking attribute of the Supreme Court in its seminal period was its emergence "full-blown" as a major factor in the political, social, and economic development of the new nation.

[19] John Randall, address to the Faculty of the Law School of the University of Chicago, Fall, 1959.

[20] See especially, Floyd E. McCaffree, "The Nomination and Confirmation of Justices of the Supreme Court of the United States, 1789–1849" (unpublished doctoral dissertation, University of Michigan, 1938).

The personal experience of a tough, persistent seaman portrays clearly the impact of this new political institution in the formative years of the Republic. When Gideon Olmstead initiated the first legal action for the prize money for the sloop *Active*,[21] he went to a state court of admiralty. This legal forum was a practical and logical choice in the late 1770s. When Olmstead successfully appealed to the only "national" tribunal available, the Court of Appeals in Cases of Capture created under the Confederation Congress, the state admiralty court refused to carry out its decree. When, in turn, the appropriate committee of the Confederation Congress supported the "national" court's ruling, the legislature of Pennsylvania ordered the state court to ignore the Congressional committee resolution. Its position prevailed.

Over a decade after the creation of the Supreme Court, Gideon tried again. His technically successful effort to challenge the old ruling of the state admiralty court before a federal district court did not win him the prize money immediately. District Judge Peters had refrained from carrying out his own ruling when the Pennsylvania legislature enacted a law defying the Olmstead ruling. By 1808, Olmstead, now 82 years old, took the issue to the Supreme Court. In the following year the Court, in an opinion by Marshall, upheld federal judicial power. The governor of Pennsylvania called out the state militia to prevent enforcement of the court decree. The confrontation between the militia and the U.S. Marshal who called a posse to help him serve process attested not only to the continued strength of an older conception of states' rights but also to the emerging significance of the new judicial branch of government. The uncertainty over the precise role of the newly created federal judiciary was underscored both by District Judge Peters and by the Commander of the resisting state militia, General Bright. Peters had originally refrained from enforcing obedience to his own court ruling from "prudential more than other motives." Bright and his militiamen were pardoned by President Madison after being fined and imprisoned for forcibly resisting a federal marshal because, in the President's words, "they had acted under a mistaken sense of duty."

The Olmstead prize-money issue, which spanned over three decades of the formative period, is illustrative of the confusion over the

[21] For a full discussion in greater detail of the tortuous legal experiences of Gideon Olmstead see John R. Schmidhauser (ed.), *Constitutional Law in the Political Process* (Chicago: Rand, McNally and Company, 1963), pp. 36–41.

Court's role that existed among contemporaries in the early part of the 19th century. Modern scholars similarly are sharply divided over conceptions of the Court's institutional role and its relation to other institutions. Consider, for example, William Nisbet Chambers' conception of the role of political parties as (a) prime contributors to nation-building, (b) shapers of government policy and mobilizers of public sentiment, (c) recruiters of party leaders and elective and appointative personnel, and (d) contributors to the political socialization or education of the American people.[22] Although Chambers does not claim that these functions belong exclusively to political parties, he fails to make even passing reference to the possibility that all but the third could, with much historical justification, be related to federal Supreme Court institutional development as well. This argument, it should be stressed, does not stem from disciplinary chauvinism but is in the nature of an appeal for a greater effort to discover possible linkages that may clarify many basic questions relating to the special institutional role of the Supreme Court.

Because certain kinds of conflicts have recurred throughout the history of the Court, an assessment of the nature and sources of such conflicts and of modern scholarly interpretation of such conflicts may prove helpful.

SOURCES OF CONGRESS–SUPREME COURT CONFLICT

C. Herman Pritchett offered one explanation for the recurring Congressional criticism of the Supreme Court by pointing out that "the American system of government has developed in such a way as to place responsibilities upon the Court which inevitably make it the subject of controversy, and bring it into conflict with the other two branches of government."[23] This contention is similar to the position of de Tocqueville, who observed more than a century ago that hardly a political issue arose in the United States that was not converted into a legal question and taken to the Court for decision.

[22] William N. Chambers, "Party Development and the American Mainstream," in William Nisbet Chambers and Walter Dean Burnham, *The American Party Systems: Stages of Political Development* (New York: Oxford University Press, 1967), pp. 7–8.

[23] C. Herman Pritchett, *Congress versus the Supreme Court* (Minneapolis, Minnesota: University of Minnesota Press, 1961), p. 5.

As former Solicitor Archibald Cox has pointed out, the source of "controversies is the peculiar nature of the Supreme Court's business."[24]

Furthermore, the responsibilities, powers, and relationships of the Court and other political institutions are never static or established once and for all. They are "evolving and changing over time in response to altered social conditions and shifts in social values and to public demands that accompany these changes."[25] The ongoing interaction between the two systems in this developmental process hardly could be free of institutional conflict.

An implicit recognition of potential conflict is apparent in the proposals, some by the justices themselves, that the Court consciously avoid certain controversial issues. If one accepts this position, it is difficult to envision the Court fulfilling its constitutional and statutory responsibilities in a positive, meaningful way, for: "If the Courts choose to avoid conflict with the legislative branch, it is inevitable that the judiciary hold a subordinate position among political institutions."[26] This contradicts the tradition that the constitutional system should be a going concern with a working interaction of the President, Congress, and Court without interpretative supremacy asserted by any one institution.

The "hands-off" policy also suggests that for certain problems there is in effect no remedy. It is doubtful that this policy could eliminate criticism. On the contrary, it would likely induce criticism from other sources, those seeking a governmental solution to what they perceive to be existing wrongs.[27] In an era characterized by rapid political and social change, such an acknowledgement of inability to participate actively in the governmental process of problem-solving would be likely to tarnish the Court's image in the minds of many who would argue that by inaction it sanctioned continuance of recognized wrongs. In the "one man, one vote" case, by pointing out the deficiencies of malapportionment but then acknowledging a supposed inability to enter the "political thickets," the Court hardly avoided conflict or instilled confidence.

[24] Archibald Cox, *The Warren Court* (Cambridge, Massachusetts: Harvard University Press, 1968), p. 1.

[25] Max Freedman, William Beaney, and Eugene U. Rostow, *Perspectives on the Court* (Evanston, Illinois: Northwestern University Press, 1967), p. 35.

[26] William J. Keefe and Morris S. Ogul, *The American Legislative Process* (Englewood Cliffs, New Jersey: Prentice-Hall, 1968), p. 472.

[27] Not to mention the Court's professional critics; see, for example, the series by Fowler Harper in the *Pennsylvania Law Review* during the past decade.

The "hands-off" approach encounters a further difficulty because it is, in and of itself, a policy decision. It is difficult to support the contention that the Supreme Court's decision in *Brown* v. *the Board of Education* was any more political than its decision in *Plessy* v. *Ferguson.* In the latter case, the Court was ratifying a policy of segregation. "Why should the process of ratification or legitimation be regarded as intrinsically less political than the process of nullification or reversal?"[28] In both the segregation and the apportionment cases it has been suggested that objections were made not because the Court had made policy, but rather because the Justices had made bad policy.[29] It goes without saying that the supporters of the Court's position in *Brown* and *Baker* were just as convinced of the correctness of the Court's decisions and its authority to make them as the critics were convinced of their incorrectness.

If the very nature of the Supreme Court's position in the federal system brings it into potential conflict with the Congress, it is difficult to conceive that the Taney Court might have shielded itself from severe criticism by taking an opposite position in the *Dred Scott case.* As long as groups and individuals have access to the institutions of government, they will follow the route most promising of success. A recent example of this pattern is the strategy taken by American organized labor. During the early 1930s labor found Congress and not the Court amenable to its program. During the postwar period, when Congress became more hostile, labor turned to the Court for support. There is little doubt that the Supreme Court will continue to be deeply involved in this struggle for power. As Walter Murphy so aptly points out:

> Recognizing the potential threat to their own policy aims which the authority of the High Bench poses, members of Congress will continue to view judicial power with a suspicion which will turn to hostility whenever they themselves or articulate segments of their constituencies disapprove of specific decisions, or when those officials fear that their own policy-making prerogatives are being threatened. The issues generating conflict may change, but the Court in the future is likely to remain as it has been in the past—a focal point in the struggle for political power.[30]

[28] Donald P. Kommers, "Professor Kurland, the Supreme Court, and Political Science," *Journal of Public Law*, Vol. 15, No. 2, 1966, p. 235.

[29] Martin Shapiro, *Law and Politics in the Supreme Court* (Chicago, Illinois: University of Chicago, 1962), p. 268.

[30] Walter Murphy, *Congress and the Supreme Court* (Chicago, Illinois: University of Chicago, 1962), p. 268.

This is not to suggest that the Supreme Court should not approach major constitutional issues cautiously and be wary of disagreeing with the branches and levels of government. "The Supreme Court has an obligation to be humble but not to the point of denying to the nation the guidance on basic democratic problems which its unique situation equips it to provide."[31] This analysis of conflicts between Congress and the Supreme Court accepts the position that, as a co-equal institution within the federal system, the Supreme Court has a positive role to play in the problem-solving process of federal governmental institutions.

> In short, the Court would become what it would in operation. And what it became was an effective and sometimes aggressive instrument of policy making, interacting with the legislative and executive branches under conditions of constructive or creative tensions.[32]

The convergence of interest in developmental political analysis by historians and political scientists in the area of political parties suggests that similar emphasis upon what V. O. Key referred to as the "dimension of time"[33] is in order in judicial-legislative studies. If we examine constitutional and political historical development, can we say that the major political parties develop and maintain consistent and clearly identifiable positions relating to the Supreme Court and the federal judiciary? Were Jeffersonians and Jacksonian Democrats generally suspicious, if not openly antagonistic to the Supreme Court, particularly until 1850? Were Whigs and Republicans generally staunch defenders, with the exception of the Civil War and Reconstruction eras?[34] Or were the partisans of each successive era "pragmatic"—did they support or oppose the federal judiciary as it suited their particular public policy objectives? Stanley I. Kutler's reappraisal of the historical interpretations of James G. Randall, Charles Warren, and William A. Dunning underscores the problem of definitive evaluation of historic data. Kutler's effort at reappraisal was still essentially an attempt to trace

[31] C. Herman Pritchett, *The Political Offender and the Warren Court* (Boston, Massachusetts: Boston University Press, 1958), p. 73—7a, 7b.

[32] Kommers, *op. cit.*, p. 241.

[33] Chambers and Burnham, *op. cit.*, p. vii.

[34] For a good summary of a variety of historians' interpretations of party attitudes toward the Supreme Court see Stanley I. Kutler, *Judicial Power and Reconstruction Politics* (Chicago, Illinois: University of Chicago Press, 1968), pp. 4–49.

partisan conflict. Although Kutler occasionally refers to the overall institutional role of the Court, the material upon which his conclusions are based generally comprises conventional historical accounts of partisan battles. He did not employ systematic comparative analyses of Congressional roll-call divisions in the antebellum, Civil War, and Reconstruction Congresses. At times his failure to utilize the totality of Congress–Court interactions created serious problems of interpretation. A comparison of some research findings and conclusions of Stanley I. Kutler and Gerald Jordan illustrate the point. Kutler concluded that

> It is apparent that the congressional threat to the federal judiciary during the Reconstruction era has been grossly exaggerated. . . .
>
> During the Civil War and Reconstruction period Congress significantly enlarged federal jurisdiction. The fifteen years following the outbreak of Civil War, indeed, witnessed the greatest legislative expansion of jurisdiction since 1789. In a variety of ways, such as additional federal court power to issue writs of habeas corpus, new jurisdiction in admiralty and bankruptcy, and a broader scope for Supreme Court review by writs of error, the federal system was given authority to assume a more dominant position over the state courts.[35]

However, in his comparative study of the Dutch and the American judicial systems (dealing with the World War II and Civil War eras, respectively), Jordan argued that the function of legitimizing the collective decisional process cannot be performed unless the judiciary possesses an "image of legitimacy."[36] Such an image was difficult to maintain in the face of Presidential–Congressional actions such as that involving the federal circuit judges for the District of Columbia. When these judges, presiding over the second highest court in the nation, applied Chief Justice Taney's doctrine of the *Merryman case* by initiating habeas corpus proceedings against the Provost Marshal of the District, one General Andrew Porter, the General arrested the attorney attempting to serve the order. As Jordan described it,

> Lincoln ordered [Secretary] Seward to throw a provost guard around [Chief Justice] Merrick's home on I street, hold the Judge under "protective custody," send his family to a downtown hotel,

[35] Kutler, *op. cit.*, p. 143.

[36] Gerald Jordan, "The Impact of Crises Upon Judicial Behavior," unpublished paper delivered at the annual meeting of the American Political Science Association. September, 1960, New York, p. 3.

> censor his incoming and outgoing correspondence, and keep his visitors under surveillance. To complete the action Lincoln ordered the Treasury to stop paying Merrick's salary until further notice. . . . [After the circuit court capitulated] Merrick was allowed to return to the bench, but a bill was soon introduced in Congress, ultimately passed, and signed by the President providing for the abolition of the Court. Its same functions—but not the same judges—were transferred to a new "Supreme Court for the District of Columbia."[37]

Kutler's explanation of the alleged enhancement of the Supreme Court's role is in fact an implicit recognition of the institutional aggrandizement of a particular political party and the emergence of powerful corporate interests primarily hopeful of avoiding unfriendly state judicial tribunals. As he put it,

> The Republicans, whatever their disappointment with the Dred Scott decision, recognized the Court as a desirable prize. . . . They were concerned with the Court as an instrument of power. . . .[38]

The seeming paradox that judicial institutional influence may wane while its jurisdictional authority is legislatively expanded was highlighted when the main thrust of the emergent policies of the post-Civil War era became fully apparent. The stern criticisms of the federal judiciary embodied in works such as Brooks Adams' *The Theory of Social Revolutions*,[39] the earlier political attacks of the Populists,[40] and the reform efforts of the Progressives were all manifestations of lack of confidence in the integrity and impartiality of the judiciary. James Bradley Thayer's excellent essays on the life of John Marshall contain several observations and some restrained criticisms that may serve as useful points of departure for modern research. Thayer's hypotheses concerning the impact of greater judicial activity are of interest in themselves. But they also suggest that a careful demarcation of the variety of institutional developments—judicial from political or corporate—may in turn provide more evidence of linkages between such institutional systems. Thayer suggested, for example, that

[37] Jordan, *op cit.*, pp. 36, 38; interestingly enough this episode is not reported or discussed in Kutler's work.

[38] Kutler, *op cit.*, p. 162; for his discussions of corporate influence see pp. 143–160.

[39] New York: MacMillan Company, 1913.

[40] Alan Westin, "The Supreme Court, the Populist Movement, and the Campaign of 1896," *15 Journal of Politics* (February, 1953), pp. 3–41.

courts, by readily assuming greater power over state legislative acts, contributed to decreased public confidence and interest in state legislatures:

> The people, all this while, become careless as to whom they send to the legislature; too often they cheerfully vote for men whom they would not trust with an important private affair, and when these unfit persons are found to pass foolish and bad laws, and the courts step in and disregard them, the people are glad that these wiser gentlemen on the bench are so ready to protect them against their more immediate representatives.[41]

With respect to the federal judiciary Thayer argued that

> Great and, indeed, inestimable as are the advantages in a popular government of this conservative influence—the power of the judiciary to disregard unconstitutional legislation—it should be remembered that the exercise of it, even when unavoidable, is always attended with a serious evil, namely, that the correction of legislative mistakes comes from the outside, and the people thus lose the political experience, and the moral education and stimulus that come from fighting the question out in the ordinary way, and correcting their own errors. . . .
>
> [After discussing two controversial Supreme Court decisions which upheld the validity of state and national legislation, Thayer conceded that this led to political divisions.] But I venture to think that the good which came to the country and its people from the vigorous thinking that had to be done in the political debates that followed, from the infiltration through every part of the population of sound ideas and sentiments, from the rousing into activity of opposite elements, the enlargement of ideas, the strengthening of moral fibre, and the growth of political experience that came out of it—that all this far more than outweighed any evil which ever flowed from the refusal of the court to interfere with the work of the legislature . . .
>
> The tendency of a common and easy resort to this great function, now lamentably too common, is to dwarf the political capacity of the people, and to deaden its sense of moral responsibility.[42]

It is an interesting commentary on the state of the art and science of political science that the challenging hypothesis of Thayer concerning the impact of judicial institutional development upon other

[41] James Bradley Thayer, *John Marshall* (Boston: Houghton, Mifflin and Company, 1901), p. 104.
[42] *Ibid.*, pp. 106–107.

public or private institutions and practices has not been investigated empirically. We do indeed know, as Elmer Schattschneider dramatically sketched it,[43] that the era Thayer described did experience a tremendous decline in public participation in voting. No hard data provide evidence of a linkage between these developments. Subsequent investigation utilizing Polsby's conception of institutional development may provide at least the preliminary research foundation from which broader explorations of institutional interaction may be launched.

[43] Elmer E. Schattschneider, *The Semisovereign People: A Realist's View of Democracy in America* (New York: Holt, Rinehart and Winston, 1960).

4

The Institutionalization of Congress and the Supreme Court

From the perspective of social background, age, and sex, individuals who served in the Congress and on the Supreme Court seem remarkably similar. Few women have served in Congress; none has served on the Supreme Court. Relatively few members of underprivileged ethnic minorities have served in the House and Senate, although the number of blacks, American Indians, and Mexican-Americans has increased slightly in recent years. Only recently did the first black, Thurgood Marshall, become an Associate Justice. No American Indian or Mexican-American has been chosen in the entire history of the Court. The general coincidence of social characteristics finds a concomitant in respect to age. The authors of one widely used American government textbook began an analysis of the recruitment of members of Congress with the following statement: "Perhaps the most noticeable characteristic of congressmen is that they are, by and large, older men."[1] This description would, of course, also provide an apt characterization of the Supreme Court and the federal judiciary. Harvey C. Lehman, in his study of *Age and Achievement*, found that there is a general "upward shift in the ages of leaders" in

[1] Marion D. Irish and James W. Prothro, *The Politics af American Democracy*, 4th ed. (Englewood Cliffs, New Jersey: Prentice-Hall, Inc., 1968), p. 337.

contrast to a downward shift in the age of achievement of "scientific and other creative contributions."[2] In his initial study of political leaders published in 1947, Lehman developed a table describing longitudinal changes in the Senate and House of Representatives through 1925.[3] Although the data collected were not organized in identical fashion, some general graphic comparisons may be made of his material on national legislators with data relating to the age at which members of the federal judiciary took their oaths of office.

FIGURE 4-1. Comparison of chronological ages of the members of Congress and Justices of the Supreme Court and Judges of the U.S. Courts of Appeals.

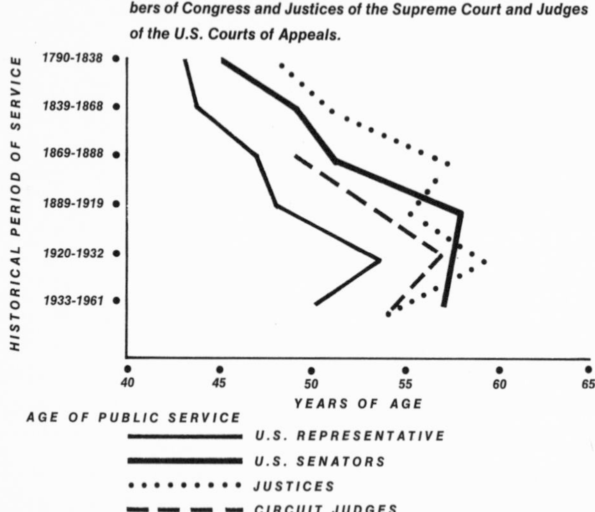

Figure 4-1 indicates that the chronological age patterns for members of the House and Senate (1799–1965) and justices of the Supreme Court (1789–1961) and judges of the U.S. Courts of Appeals (1869–1961) were generally similar.[4]

[2] Harvey C. Lehman, *Age and Achievement* (Princeton: Princeton University Press, 1953), p. 288.

[3] Items taken from Table I of Harvey C. Lehman, "The Ages of Eminent Leaders: Then and Now," *52 American Journal of Sociology* (January, 1947), p. 343.

[4] The data for the justices and judges were derived from John R. Schmidhauser, "Age and Judicial Behavior: American Higher Appellate Judges," in Wilma Donahue and Clark Tibbitts, *Politics of Age* (Ann Arbor: University of Michigan, 1962), pp. 109–110. The data utilized to update Lehman's periodic analysis of the ages of senators and representatives were derived from *21 Congressional Quarterly Almanac: 89th Congress, 1st session* (Washington: Congressional Quarterly Service, 1966), p. 33.

Given the consonance of some of the attributes of members of Congress and the Justices, what differentiates them? If the general tendency has been toward the recruitment of older persons in both kinds of institutions, what factors can be identified as influential in the recruitment process?

Here Ralph K. Huitt's emphasis upon the significance of institutions is pertinent, particularly in terms of his definition. The term "institution" connoted, according to Huitt, "a pattern of behavior of great stability and predictability, including the expectations people have that the pattern will be maintained."[5] The manner in which individuals gain seats in the House and Senate is, to put it mildly, considerably different in kind from the process of selection of members of the Supreme Court. To be sure, both selection processes reflect the influence of political factors, but the processes by which Presidents choose members of the Supreme Court generally resemble sedate rituals in comparison with the rough and tumble of congressional campaigning. Matthews contends that it is difficult to understand how and why senators act "without considering what happens to them while they are running for office."[6] Few seriously entertain the myth that the judicial office seeks the man, although the notion is assiduously cultivated in some professional legal circles. But the judicial selection process in modern times does not generally expose potential justices to the kind of importuning commonplace in congressional campaigning. For membership on the Supreme Court, qualitative factors have characteristically been important, although political party, ideological predilections, religion, interest group affiliations, and regional background have generally had significance. Geographic considerations were implied by the very nature of the original relationship between judicial circuits, the size of the Supreme Court, and the regional background of the early justices.[7]

Political reprisals or the threat of them figure so largely in the day-to-day lives of members of Congress that it has often been assumed

[5] Huitt, *op. cit.*, p. 11.

[6] Donald R. Matthews, *U.S. Senators and Their World* (New York: Random House, 1960), p. 68.

[7] For a full account of the relationship between Supreme Court appointments and the organization of the inferior federal courts under the Judiciary Act of 1789 and subsequent statutes in the 19th century see Floyd E. McCaffree, "The Nomination and Confirmation of Justices of the Supreme Court of the United States, 1789–1849" (Ann Arbor: unpublished doctoral dissertation, 1938).

that Supreme Court justices were immune from the cruder forms of political combat. The constitutional provisions protecting judicial independence do, indeed, provide life tenure on good behavior. The justices are obviously not subjected to the ultimate in political reprisals, defeat at the polls, a consideration of utmost importance to members of Congress. But the ingenuity of antagonistic congressmen in devising antijudicial reprisals deserves recognition in its historical and its contemporary manifestations.

In the period from 1789 through much of the antebellum era, the very conditions of national public service, whether legislative or judicial, put a premium upon recruitment of relatively young men. James Sterling Young's characterization of the Congress in the early Washington political community as one marked by "instability of membership; the constant circulation of short-time servers through the community" implicitly stressed those attributes which only the younger legislator generally possessed.[8] Although the justices enjoyed life tenure on good behavior, certain political reprisals wielded by occasional Congressional majorities taxed the vigor of the elderly. A particularly good example is provided by Whig political manipulation of the judicial circuits during the judicial tenure of Associate Justice Peter V. Daniel (1841–1860). Although the Whigs failed to prevent his senatorial confirmation in 1841, they did, in the following year, succeed in realigning the circuits. As a consequence, Justice Daniel's old circuit, comprising North Carolina and Virginia, was abolished. A new circuit, the Ninth, was created consisting of Arkansas and Mississippi. Prior to the change of 1842, Chief Justice Taney traveled only 458 miles to cover his circuit, while Daniel's predecessor, Justice McKinley would have traveled 10,000 miles to cover his. In 1844, burdened by the difficulties of annual trips from Washington to Arkansas and Mississippi, Daniel wrote former President Martin Van Buren:

> I am here [Jackson, Mississippi] two thousand miles from home (calculating by the travel record) on the pilgrimage by an exposure to which, it was the calculation of savage malignity that I had been driven from the Bench. Justice to my friends, and a determination to defeat the machinations of mine and of their enemies, have decided me to undergo the experiment, and I have done so at no

[8] James Sterling Young, *The Washington Community: 1800–1828* (New York: Columbia University Press, 1966), pp. 98, 87–109, and 143–153.

small hazard through air of fever at Vicksburg and convulsive and autumnal fevers in this place and vicinity.[9]

The burdens of circuit duty were viewed seriously by Presidents intent on filling vacancies with men who would remain on the Court for long tenure. As Charles Fairman put it,

It was important then to select a man whose bones would knit if he chanced to be thrown from his carriage as he made his progress over rutty highways.[10]

Biographical data indicate that the average appointment age of members of the Supreme Court was 48 in the period from 1790 to 1838 and 51 in the succeeding period, in both cases below the average appointment age after the justices were relieved of circuit duty.[11] It is clear that the relationship between a Congressionally imposed circuit duty for members of the Supreme Court and age was, as a matter of fact, argued as an issue of institutional performance during the period before the Civil War. Daniel Webster, in the judiciary debates of 1823–1824, argued that:

The Supreme Court is, itself, in some measure, insulated, it has not frequent occasions of contact with the community. The Bar that attends it is neither numerous nor regular in its attendance. . . . If the Judges of the Supreme Court, therefore, are wholly withdrawn from the circuits, it appears to me there is a danger of leaving them without the means of useful intercourse with other judicial characters, with the profession of which they are members, and with the public. . . . I think it useful that Judges should see in practice the operation and effect of their own decisions. This will prevent theory from running too far, or refining too much.[12]

A few years earlier in 1819, Senator Truman Lacock of Pennsylvania had presented a direct political appeal for retention of circuit duty, linking age and purported ideological and institutional purposes. Lacock contended that the elimination of circuit duty would

[9] John P. Frank, *Justice Daniel Dissenting: A Biography of Peter V. Daniel, 1784–1860* (Cambridge, Massachusetts: Harvard University Press, 1964), p. 276.

[10] Charles Fairman, "The Retirement of Federal Judges," *51 Harvard Law Review* (1937–1938), p. 404.

[11] See John R. Schmidhauser, "Age and Judicial Behavior: American Higher Appellate Judges," *op. cit.*, Table 5, p. 109.

[12] Charles Warren, *II The Supreme Court in United States History* (Boston: Little, Brown and Company, 1922), p. 138.

mean that the justices would be subjected to "dangerous influences and strong temptations that might bias their minds and pollute the stream of national justice." He attempted to justify this conclusion as follows:

> You will have not only your Judges but your attorneys confined to the City of Washington. The Judges are to be old men when appointed, and the infirmities of old age will every day increase, and as the useful and vigorous faculties of their minds diminish, in the same proportion will their obstinancy and vanity increase. Old men are often impatient of contradiction, frequently vain and susceptable of flattery. These weaknesses incident to old age will be discovered and practised upon by the lawyer willing to make the most of his profession, and located in the same city, holding daily and familiar intercourse with the Judges. And thus, your Court may become subservient to the Washington Bar. The Judges, bowed down by the weight of years, will be willing to find a staff to lean upon; and the opinion of the Washington Bar is made the law of the land. A knot of attorneys at or near the seat of government having gained the ear, and secured the confidence of the court, will banish all competition from abroad. . . . The distributive justice of the nation may be subjected to the control of a combination of Washington lawyers.[13]

The materials of constitutional history abound with tantalizing commentaries relating the ages of political leaders to concepts of institutional development. It is essential, however, that these historical materials be evaluated to distinguish the idiosyncratic or anecdotal from data rigorously classifiable for general descriptive or explanatory purposes. It is here that the methods of sociologists and gerontologists may provide powerful assistance to the interpretation of broad institutional changes such as "The Aging of the House."[14]

THE INSTITUTIONALIZATION OF THE HOUSE OF REPRESENTATIVES AND THE FEDERAL JUDICIARY

Nelson Polsby, in an exploratory investigation of the institutionalization of the House of Representatives, identified three major charac-

[13] *Ibid.*, pp. 134–135.

[14] The phrase is that of T. Richard Witmer, "The Aging of the House," *79 Political Science Quarterly* (1964), pp. 526–541.

teristics of institutionalized organizations. These comprised (a) the establishment and maintenance of boundaries that differentiate a particular institution from others, (b) the specialization of functions within the institution, and (c) the evolution of standardized institutional procedures and ethical norms. In his analysis of the third characteristic, Polsby summed up the process as follows: "Precedents and rules are followed; merit systems replace favoritism and nepotism; and impersonal codes supplant personal preferences as prescriptions for behavior."[15] This particular characterization of the process of institutionalization provides a useful point of departure for analysis of the Congress and the Supreme Court.

The choice of the ethical norms adopted in the process of institutional development is generally viewed as one of the fundamental problems confronting either a particular society or a total civilization. This viewpoint is exemplified in descriptive studies such as that of George Graham, who observed, in his study of the early 1950s, that morals and politics "are linked, and both are fundamental in modern civilization."[16] Similarly, Gerald Jordan's comment that a judiciary cannot perform the "function of legitimation" unless it possesses an "image of legitimacy"[17] presumably would have relevance for either a legislature or a judiciary. Each individual entering public service is, of course, the produce of his family, community, and overall social environment. But the process of political and/or judicial socialization, by its very nature, places the individual within the framework of certain institutional expectations that may have a decisive influence on his behavior as a public official. Thus Polsby's approach is particularly important, even though its application to institutions such as the Supreme Court and the Congress presents difficult research problems. First, most historical accounts of these institutions provide anecdotal rather than systematic treatments of the material most relevant to such an exploration. Second, Polsby's research experience with the House of Representatives applies with even greater relevance to this broader undertaking. As he put it, "Simple operational indices of institutional complexity and univer-

[15] Nelson W. Polsby, "The Institutionalization of the U.S. House of Representatives," *62 American Political Science Review* (March, 1968), p. 145.

[16] George A. Graham, *Morality in American Politics* (New York: Random House, 1952), p. vii.

[17] Gerald Jordan, "The Impact of Crises upon Judicial Behavior" (unpublished paper delivered at the annual meeting of the American Political Science Association, September, 1960, New York City, New York), p. 3.

salistic-automated decision-making are less easy to produce in neat and comparable time series."[18] Recognizing these inherent problems, the subsequent comparative analysis must be viewed as a preliminary mapping survey, whose findings must obviously be presented as tentative.

Polsby identified three indices illustrative of the growth of internal complexity of the House of Representatives: (a) the growth in autonomy and importance of committees, (b) the growth in the specialized agencies of party leadership, and (c) the general increase in auxiliary aids and emoluments of various kinds. Although this approach and the indices may be deemed appropriate to the study of a legislature, other indices of institutional development are needed to indicate the maturation of judicial institutional characteristics.

In its historical development, the House of Representatives experienced remarkable changes in institutional characteristics. For example, the evolution of institutional distinctiveness characterized by the establishment of boundaries was a slow process during the early years of the new nation. Omitting the Congress of 1789, when all members were first-termers, the turnover of House members exceeded 50% in 15 elections between 1790 and 1882. By contrast, after 1946, the turnover of House members exceeded 20% only twice.[19]

In addition, the evolution of ethical norms for both legislative and judicial institutions deserves full analysis. Among the recent systematic empirical investigations of the informal norms of legislative behavior, the contributions of Allan Kornberg provided the clearest and most perceptive recognition of the institutional significance of standards of ethical conduct. Kornberg explicitly described the functions served by "the rules of the game" in the Canadian House of Commons as follows: "(1) to expedite the flow of legislative business, (2) to channel and mitigate conflict, (3) to defend members against external criticism." The latter function was, according to Kornberg, necessitated by the reality or prospect of outside attack; indeed, external criticism tended "to promote legislative solidarity regardless of party, and establish norms designed to discourage behavior which might bring the system and its members under attack from outsiders."[20]

[18] Polsby, *op. cit.*, p. 153.

[19] Polsby, *op. cit.*, p. 146.

[20] Allan Kornberg, "The Rules of the Game in the Canadian House of Commons," *26 Journal of Politics* (May, 1964), pp. 359, 361.

Through much of the literature of law and political science there is a tendency to impute high institutional standards of ethical behavior to judicial institutions and relatively low ones to legislatures. A striking and illustrative example of the contrast is provided by Karl Llewellyn's essay on "The American Common Law Tradition and American Democracy," portions of which were quoted in Chapter 2, and H. Hubert Wilson's *Congress: Corruption and Compromise.*[21] Llewellyn provided an exceptionally perceptive portrait of the institutionalized "craft tradition" of higher appellate courts as it has emerged in the middle of the 20th century. Wilson's work emphasizes, with modern examples, the generally accepted notion that congressional standards in ethical matters are rather loose, a viewpoint reiterated in a number of recent textbooks on the subject.[22] More systematically, J. Willard Hurst undertook, in his seminal *Growth of American Law*, an appraisal of the evolution of institutional characteristics of legislatures and judiciaries in America. He observed that,

> Definite standards of ethical behavior for the bench crystallized in the nineteenth century, whatever the varying practical effect in different levels of courts. As late as mid-twentieth century, no comparably definite ideal had become set for the legislature.[23]

Hurst also pinpointed one area in which traditionally accepted autonomy in the development of institutional procedures is denied the Supreme Court and the federal judiciary. Hurst argued that,

> History and precedent offer substantial support for the inherent power of Anglo-American courts to make rules for procedure in cases that come before them. Nonetheless, statutory authorization was obtained before the Supreme Court of the United States promulgated rules for procedure in various types of proceedings in the federal courts.[24]

[21] Karl N. Llewellyn, "The American Common Law Tradition and American Democracy," 1, *Journal of Legal and Political Sociology* (October, 1942), p. 32, and H. Hubert Wilson, *Congress: Corruption and Compromise* (New York: Rinehart and Co., 1951).

[22] See, for example, William J. Keefe and Morris S. Ogul, *The American Legislative Process: Congress and the States*, 2nd edition (Englewood Cliffs, N.J.: Prentice-Hall, Inc. 1968), pp. 5–11.

[23] James Willard Hurst, *The Growth of American Law* (Boston: Little, Brown and Company, 1950), p. 63.

[24] *Ibid.*, pp. 75–76.

Hurst did not, however, comment upon the full implications of congressional power to allocate or refrain from allocating money for the federal courts. The Supreme Court of the United States is the most powerful judicial body in the world if power is defined as successful invocation of the power of judicial review. Yet, ironically, if measured by another standard, the Supreme Court is weaker than a state District Court in Iowa because the latter, like its counterparts in several other states, continues to exercise the traditional inherent power not only over court procedure but over judicial appropriations as well. While Congress continues to deal parsimoniously with the Supreme Court, judges of the Iowa District Court in Johnson County, for example, merely send the bills for the reconstruction of a court facility to their "legislators," the county supervisors, *without prior authorization.* The supervisors, although they may grumble privately, pay the bills without the mildest public display of displeasure.[25]

The point of this cursory comparison is not to make an overdrawn claim of the alleged superiority of a state court of original jurisdiction over the most prestigious judicial body in the world. It is to show the necessity for thorough exploration of every facet of institutional interrelationship to provide a more balanced portrait. By this standard, what were the characteristics of legislative and judicial institutionalization predominant in the major historical periods of America's growth as a modern nation? How, for example, did the institutional standards of higher appellate courts develop? Did changes in institutional expectations coincide with striking changes in the attitudes of new political generations? Relating those questions to a specific institutional issue for illustrative purposes, we may ask what was expected of the new Supreme Court by its political architects—the designers of the Constitution of 1787. In terms of institutional modes of operation, was there a sharp distinction between the "political" branches of the federal government and the judicial in

[25] For example, in an interview on August 25, 1969, Johnson County Auditor Dolores Rogers cited a recent situation in which a state district judge, when apprised of a mild reluctance on the part of the supervisors regarding an unanticipated judicial cost, silenced them with the comment that if you "don't do it, I'll order it!" For a general description of the powers of Iowa County supervisors see Jacob Van Ek, "The County Board of Supervisors," in Benjamin F. Shambaugh (ed.), *County Government and Administration in Iowa*, which comprises volume IV in the Iowa Applied History Series (Iowa City: Iowa State Historical Society, 1925), pp. 19–76.

the formative years? Is there a firm historical basis for the sort of institutional diversity presently attributed to the Congress and the Supreme Court?

As was detailed in Chapter 3, Charles Warren's research indicated that prior to the adoption of the constitution of 1787, a clearcut distinction between judicial, legislative, and executive functions did not exist either in the governmental institutions of Great Britain or in the variety of colonial governments developed under the aegis of the mother country.

Interestingly enough, the stages in the institutional growth of the House of Representatives, which according to Polsby's analysis represented progressive development of institutional autonomy and complexity, did not, when measured against Hurst's findings, bring the consequences described by Polsby. Polsby argues, for example, that "along with the more obvious effects of institutionalization, the process has also served to increase the power of the House within the political system. . . ."[26] This conclusion is difficult to reconcile with Hurst's finding that

> The years 1750 to 1820 offered legislators a chance to become the principal lawmakers for the nation as a whole and also for the states . . . as we go on the story of the legislature becomes negative in the telling.

Hurst pointed out that the legislature began, in the post-colonial period, with "an impressive trinity of advantages." These were (a) its legitimacy in public opinion, (b) its broad grant of constitutional authority, and (c) its power as "the grand inquest of the nation and the states to inquire into matters of public concern." Yet by the 1870s, the courts emerged as major influences. As Hurst put it, "between 1820 and 1890 the judges were already taking the initiative in lawmaking." He also stressed that "through the injunction and the receivership, judges anticipated the later role of executive and administrative agencies." As this comment indicated, Hurst concluded that initiative finally passed to the executive and administrative branches.[27]

Hurst's recognition that while standards of ethical conduct had been adopted by the higher appellate judges of the nation and the states, no similar development had taken place in the legislatures

[26] Polsby, *op. cit.*, p. 166.
[27] Hurst, *op. cit.*, pp. 23–24; 85.

has been the focus of a good deal of speculative comment. It has been suggested that the institutional standards of appellate courts are in part a natural feature of a legal profession which in the early 19th century was limited to "gentlemen." Indeed, there were few universally accepted standards for admission to the bar in the period in which the American appellate courts were developing. The virtual limitation of law practice to "gentlemen," it was argued, made it unnecessary to police the dishonorable for, in theory at least, "gentlemen" were by definition honorable. For example, the sons of wealthy plantation owners entering public life in antebellum South Carolina were provided, if they studied at the University of South Carolina, with a book of admonitions concerning the ethical obligations of public officials. In 1830 Francis Lieber published the first edition of his *Manual of Political Ethics*. The title page carried the additional comment that the work was "designed for the use of Colleges and Students at Law."[28]

The major difficulty with the so-called gentry-class explanation of the evolution of ethical standards in the American appellate courts is the fact that the historical evidence is rather contradictory. The infamous Yazoo Land Fraud is often cited as a particularly horrendous example of venality on the part of legislators. In a period of little over a week, the Georgia legislature disposed of over thirty-five million acres of public land, comprising a substantial portion of the present-day states of Alabama and Mississippi, for the price of less than a penny and a half per acre. The four land speculation companies involved were assisted not only by several state legislative leaders, but by prominent state and federal judges as well. Beveridge, in his account of the events of 1795, documented the fact that a member of the Supreme Court was among those speculating in the land. Judge William Smith of the Georgia Superior Court earned thirteen thousand dollars as a lobbyist for the measure, and Federal District Judge Nathaniel Pendleton actually participated in the bribing of state legislators to secure their votes.[29]

Although it would be inaccurate to generalize from a single instance, it is clear that many of the self-policing rules and traditions of modern appellate courts were not developed by the late 18th and

[28] Francis Lieber, *Manual of Political Ethics* (London: J. B. Lippincott Company, 1892).

[29] Albert J. Beveridge, *III The Life of John Marshall* (Boston: Houghton Mifflin Company, 1919), pp. 546–602.

early 19th centuries. As Secretary of State, John Marshall was at least technically responsible for the events about which he ruled as Chief Justice in *Marbury* v. *Madison*. The tradition of self-disqualification would have inhibited his participation in such a case in modern times. The years of political attack which buffeted the federal judiciary and later many of the state appellate courts served to develop a keener awareness of the need for institutionalization of ethical standards. Marshall himself contributed to this tradition, as did his controversial successor, Roger Brooke Taney. Despite the harsh indictment of some of his contemporaries, Chief Justice Taney, a slaveholder and member of the Southern gentry at the time of his appointment, clearly maintained a sense of his institutional responsibility that overrode his personal view on the great regional crisis that resulted in the Civil War.[30] So strong has the judicial tradition of institutional responsibility become that Judge W. Calvin Chesnut, commenting on the malfeasance of Circuit Judge Martin Manton, could convey with certainty the universality of the institutional expectations underpinning Judge Manton's conviction and imprisonment in the federal penitentiary at Lewisburgh, Pennsylvania. Judge Chesnut summarized this conception in this manner:

> . . . all public office is a public trust; but the judicial office is even more than that—it is a sacred trust. It is abhorrent to our conception of public justice that a judge should be influenced by the idea of personal profit in deciding the controversies of other people.[31]

In contrast, the much-discussed "club spirit" in the House of Representatives and in the Senate has not contributed to the development of institutional standards of ethical conduct. In fact, the conclusion must be drawn, in agreement with Hurst, that the national Congress has not kept pace with the judiciary in the development of institutional standards for such conduct. The club spirit generally is invoked to defend members rather than to enhance the prestige of the institution.

The case of Adam Clayton Powell to the contrary notwithstanding, the 20th-century evidence supports the contention of George Graham that the House of Representatives does not consider conviction for a crime (or the strong probability of such conviction) a

[30] John R. Schmidhauser, "Judicial Behavior and the Sectional Crisis of 1837–1860," *23 Journal of Politics* (November 1961), pp. 616–634.

[31] Quoted in Allan Vestal, "A Study in Perfidy," *35 Indiana Law Journal* (Fall, 1959), p. 21.

"disqualification for the high office of serving in the Congress."[32] In the 1940s and 1950s, for example, Republican Congressmen J. Parnell Thomas (New Jersey) and Walter E. Brehm (Ohio) and Democratic Congressmen James M. Curley (Mass.) and Andrew J. May (Kentucky) were convicted of sundry crimes and either fined or imprisoned. Yet none of the four was subjected to any disciplinary action by the House.

The basic problem is highlighted in the career of Daniel Webster. In the judgment of his biographer, "Webster attached perhaps an undue importance to material possessions" throughout his lifetime. Willard Hurst reports that when the renewal of the charter of the Second United States Bank came before Congress, Senator Webster wrote to the bank's president, Nicholas Biddle, a direct request for money: "I believe that my retainer has not been renewed or *refreshed* as usual. If it be wished that my relation to the Bank should be continued, it may be well to send me the usual retainer."[33]

The modern archetype is effectively described by Congressman Richard Bolling as the "hidden persuader." The "hidden persuader" is perceptively recognized by Bolling as corrupt but also "corrupted by forces that are equally culpable."[34] One of the most important analyses of these forces was made by the Douglas Committee on Ethical Standards in Government.

> The forces that would drive public servants from the straight and narrow path of virtue center chiefly upon a limited area, the area in which Government is heavily "action laden." This is the area in which there are big economic stakes, where the decisions of legislators and administrators directly affect the business, or the property, or the income of particular groups or individuals. The abuses of discretion or the exploitation of power are most serious chiefly where the Government is dispensing valuable rights and privileges, constructing extensive public works, spending vast sums for military supplies and equipment, making loans, granting direct or indirect subsidies, levying taxes, and regulating the activities of privileged monopolies or economic practices in which there is a public interest.[35]

[32] Graham, *op. cit.*, p. 89.

[33] James Willard Hurst, *The Growth of American Law* (Boston: Little, Brown and Company, 1950), p. 367.

[34] Richard Bolling, *House Out of Order* (New York: E. P. Dutton & Co., 1966), pp. 43–45.

[35] Graham, *op. cit.*, p. 29.

Recent studies of the federal judiciary indicate that the federal judges and justices have been considered appropriate targets by the same interest groups. C. Peter Magrath's excellent investigation of the background of *Fletcher* v. *Peck* documents the fact that in this case, early in the Court's history, "a large and well-organized pressure group lobbied a case to the United States Supreme Court." Ironically, until the Court decided in favor of the Yazoo purchasers, the Congress had, albeit tempestuously, resisted requests for compensation of the supposedly innocent buyers of land from the original speculators. The Court's favorable decision was effectively utilized by congressional advocates of the land speculators. By 1814, four years after the Court's decision, congressional reimbursement was granted. Joseph Story, who later served on the Court, was a paid lobbyist for the speculators. He not only "cultivated" the justices but discussed the Georgia claims directly with Chief Justice Marshall. Magrath compiled impressive evidence that *Fletcher* v. *Peck* was a collusive suit, a fact touched upon but not pursued by Justice William Johnson.[36] Yet the evidence is clear that American appellate judges, both state and federal, have, by modern times, developed rather high institutional standards of ethical conduct.

What factors have contributed to the development of such institutional standards within the higher appellate courts of the fifty states and the nation? Limiting the question somewhat, what factors contributed to such a high level of development within the federal judiciary?

Perhaps the first factor was the general commitment of the framers of the Constitution to safeguarding the members of the federal judiciary from the ordinary operation of the system of political rewards and reprisals characteristic of the era. The commitment incorporated in the Constitution for tenure on good behavior was eventually interpreted as entailing a reciprocal obligation on the part of the judges so protected. The federal judges and justices were expected to refrain from the more obvious forms of partisan activity. But it is noteworthy that a number of the more intense Federalists on the Bench were rather unrestrained in their activities, particularly in the period just before the Presidential election of 1800.

Commenting upon the first two decades of the new judicial system, Alan Westin argued that,

[36] C. Peter Magrath, *Yazoo: Law and Politics in the New Republic—The Case of Fletcher* v. *Peck* (Providence: Brown University Press, 1966), pp. vii, 50–100.

> The line between the judicial and political spheres was quite indistinct in the first days of the young Republic . . . and state judges were often open partisans. Supreme Court Justices shared this mode in the first decade or two of the nation.[37]

Westin described the political activities of the justices: e.g., the gubernatorial races of Justice William Cushing (in Massachusetts) and Chief Justice Jay (in New York) and the Presidential electioneering of Justices Samuel Chase and Bushrod Washington.

Westin might have noted that in addition to the indistinctness of the line between "judicial and political spheres" there was a similar uncertainty concerning judicial as distinct from legislative and executive functions. His comparison of federal judicial partisanship to the "open" political activity of state judges must be reappraised on this ground. Most state judges, by the nature of the system in which they operated, were expected to be partisans. In South Carolina, for example, state judges were chosen by the state legislature, and sitting legislators sometimes vied for the judicial vacancies they themselves created.[38] Operating in systems which were not, at least at the outset, prone to give much attention to the doctrine of separation of powers, the state judicial systems often developed rather independently of national judicial trends, which had implications for the relative positions of the respective judiciaries in the total political system. Chancellor James Kent, appraising the American judicial systems after several decades of national experience with the new federal judiciary, attached great importance to the influence of the "tenure on good behavior" specified by the Constitution for the federal judges and justices. In fact, he argued that there was a relationship between this factor and the quality of decision-making:

> The judiciary of the United States has an advantage over many of the State Courts, in the tenure of office of the office of the Judges, and the liberal and stable provision for their support. The United States are, by these means, fairly entitled to command better talents, and to look to more firmness of purpose, greater independence to action, and brighter displays of learning. The federal administration of justice has a manifest superiority over that of the individual states, in consequence of the uniformity of its

[37] Alan F. Westin (ed.), *An Autobiography of the Supreme Court* (New York: MacMillan Company, 1963), p. 7.

[38] Donald G. Morgan, *Justice William Johnson: The First Dissenter* (Columbia: University of South Carolina Press, 1954), pp. 35–36.

exploration, conventional historical investigations such as Carmen and Luthin's *Lincoln and Patronage* attest to the continued vitality of political partisan influences upon the federal judiciary, although they are not so direct as those bearing on the Congress.[46]

A number of the students of institutional development have argued that the greater complexity and stability of membership of particular political institutions are attributes of a kind of institutional maturation which allegedly enhances political stability.[47] One facet of this institutional tendency toward stability, argue the proponents of this hypothesis, is the professionalization of the personnel manning a particular institution. Thus congressmen and senators have, as the House and Senate have "matured," entered service in those bodies at a later stage in life than their 19th-century counterparts and have remained in these institutions for a considerably longer period. The same pattern has influenced judicial institutions.

One commonly held assumption in professional legal circles about state and federal appellate judicial institutions and the national and state legislatures relates to qualitative differences. The classic 19th-century statement of this view of state courts was made by Chancellor James Kent in his *Commentaries on American Law* previously cited.[48]

One important point to stress, however, relates to a key attribute of Congress' relationship to the Supreme Court. As recent congressional attacks on the Court have indicated, the relative status of the states' judicial institutions (to which Congress might turn if it decided to curtail the appellate jurisdiction of the Supreme Court) could be of significant importance. The higher appellate courts of the states would provide a logical alternative in periods of Congress–Court conflict. What are some of the attributes of the state courts in terms of Polsby's conception of institutionalization?

The rationale for an emphasis upon institutional prestige is discussed clearly by Walter Murphy in his analysis of the framework of judicial power. He suggested that

> Prestige is an important source of judicial power. When combined with professional reputation it can also become an important

[46] Harry J. Carmen and Reinhard H. Luthin, *Lincoln and Patronage* (New York, Columbia University Press, 1943), pp. 166–185.

[47] See Polsby, *op. cit.*, pp. 144–146, and Samuel P. Huntington, *Political Order in Changing Societies* (New Haven: Yale University Press, 1968), pp. 1–92.

[48] James Kent, op. cit., pp. 443-444.

> instrument of judicial power. Prestige refers to the Court's hold on popular esteem. Reputation refers to the judgment of other government officials about the skill and determination with which the Justices use their power to their own advantage or that of the policies they are supporting. Since public officials are likely to have been brought up to respect the judiciary as an institution, they are also likely to share to some extent the widespread belief that they *ought* to obey Supreme Court decisions. When the Justices can reinforce this feeling of obligations with professional respect for their abilities and determination, they have fashioned a very potent weapon to secure obedience and co-operation from the very people who have the physical power to ignore or even defy them.[49]

From a broader conceptual standpoint the issue raised by Murphy relates to the problems of analysis entailed in the comparative study of elite socialization. Don Searing emphasized strongly the necessity for developing variables more meaningful in intranational and cross-national research.[50] Variables categorizing public institutional emphasis and private institutional emphasis are of primary importance, particularly in clarifying problems of interpretation in intranational comparative research in the American political systems of each of the fifty states and the nation as a whole.

Of paramount importance to the study of American political and legal elites is the necessity to identify variables rigorously descriptive of individual tendencies to prefer public political institutions (courts, legislatures, administrative agencies) rather than private political institutions (corporate law firms, public relations firms, newspapers, or electronic media) for the achievement of personal career goals or ideological or political objectives.

Similarly, because ability, competence, or some similar qualitative attribute is of such great importance in professional groups, the study of legislative and judicial (or perhaps all political) elites in the United States should include a carefully defined ability or qualitative "reputation" variable. Suggested approaches to the precise development of such a variable would include the pioneering intranational measurement of judicial influence designed by Rodney Mott in the 1930s, could utilize a professional rating system such as that

[49] Walter F. Murphy, *Elements of Judicial Strategy* (Chicago: University of Chicago Press, 1954), p. 19.

[50] Donald O. Searing, "The Comparative Study of Elite Socialization," *1 Comparative Political Studies* (January, 1969), pp. 471–472, 490–491.

used by lawyers (Martindale-Hubbell), and, from historical sources, utilize peer group evaluation derived from biographical materials. The following exploration of the institutional relationships of Congress, the federal judiciary, and several state supreme Courts represents a preliminary attempt to apply these suggested variables.

Among the external factors influencing Congress-Supreme Court relations, state checks[51] on federal judicial power have figured more largely in the rhetoric of political combat than in the actual development of institutional alternatives. Thus Senator William Jenner's bill (S.2646) proposed to limit the appellate jurisdiction of the Supreme Court in several public policy areas. Among the provisions of this bill, the Supreme Court would have been denied jurisdiction to review, "either by appeal, writ of certiorari, or otherwise . . . any statute or executive regulation of any State the general purpose of which is to control subversive activities within such State. . . ."[52] The net effect of such a bill would, of course, leave final resolution of cases involving this subject matter area to the state judicial systems or, under certain circumstances, the inferior federal courts. Why, in the evolution of our political systems, has Congress refrained from developing such alternatives? Public policy considerations provide obvious explanations in some instances. However, broader institutional trends of the Congress and the Court may also be of considerable significance. What are some of the indicators of the fundamental institutional trends for nearly two centuries associated with the development of Congress and the Supreme Court?

Harvey C. Lehman's finding that there is "an upward shift in the ages of [political] leaders" in marked contrast to a downward shift in the age of achievement of "scientific and other creative contributions" provided a general framework for the specific investigation of several American appellate court systems in order to determine the extent to which the federal judiciary and several state judiciaries have experienced institutional development similar to that which Nelson Polsby described for the House of Representatives.

Data on the 92 individuals serving on the Supreme Court of the United States (1789–1961) and the 226 individuals serving on the

[51] See, for example, Walter F. Murphy and C. Herman Pritchett, *Courts, Judges, and Politics* (New York: Random House, 1961), pp. 586–592.

[52] S.2646, 85th Congress, 1st Session (1957).

federal courts of appeals (1869–1961) comprise the basic information for the federal system.[53] Fortunately, studies incorporating relatively complete age trend data by Todd Hoopes for Ohio (1800–1940), by Timothy S. Higgins for Wisconsin (1836–1949), and by Thomas A. Ewers for Iowa (1838–1961) provided useful comparative state trend information.

For the state appellate courts examined—Ohio, Wisconsin, and Iowa—there was a consistent increase in the average age at which new justices took their oaths of office, from 40 to 62 in Ohio, from 39 to 54 in Wisconsin, from and 37 to 58 in Iowa. The upward trend was not consistent in the U.S. Supreme Court and federal courts of appeals, rising from 48 to 59 and from 49 to 57 respectively from 1920 to 1932 but declining to 54 in the last period studied, 1933 to 1961. Compared to the early 19th-century record, however, all of our judicial institutions experienced an increase in the average age of oath-taking of their members. This upward shift in age of oath-taking was associated with an upward increase in the age at termination of judicial service. This rather elementary use of chronological age data is employed primarily to pinpoint the existence of changes in judicial recruitment and length of service which did not result from statutory or constitutional changes in the jurisdictions of any of those federal or state courts. Here an assessment of available biographical material provides interpretative clues. The utilization of age trend data as clues to the discovery of fundamental institutional changes was facilitated by the availability of excellent biographical source material.

J. Willard Hurst attempted, in his *Growth of American Law*, to determine historical changes in the status of public institutions—federal and state, executive, legislative, and judicial. Hurst argued that the judiciaries, both federal and state, were the unwitting beneficiaries of the loss of prestige of the state and federal legislatures. There is some evidence of marked qualitative differences in the work of the highest state appellate courts. Rodney Mott's pioneering work on "Judicial Influence" established that a few exceptional state courts, notably the Court of Appeals of New York and the Supreme Judicial Court of Massachusetts, have maintained a nation-wide reputation for decision-making excellence comparable to that of the most

[53] Schmidhauser, "Age and Judicial Behavior: American Higher Appellate Judges," *op. cit.*, pp. 109–110.

respected federal courts of appeals and the U.S. Supreme Court,[54] but many state appellate courts have not. Given the diversity of state structural (statutory and constitutional) arrangements and the more subtle differences among regional or state political cultures, it is difficult to determine what factors may be associated with these qualitative differences.

Preliminary investigation of the judicial recruitment process in Iowa suggests that the striking change in the age patterns of the state justices coincided with a concomitant qualitative change in judicial personnel. The two studies of the Iowa Supreme Court by Ewers and Wood[55] indicated a considerable shift not only in the age at oath-taking of the Iowa justices but in the characteristics of the individuals selected. In the earliest stages of its judicial recruitment, Iowa attracted a remarkable number of able young men as contestants for Supreme Court election who utilized the highest state appellate court as a stepping stone to either lucrative East Coast corporate legal practice or more important state or federal political posts. The pattern which developed after the 1880s not only ceased to produce state justices of the calibre of John Dillon of Davenport, later famous for his work on municipal law, but produced justices chosen at more advanced ages. Appointment to fill vacancies or election brought an increasing number of state justices who were elderly men at the end of the line politically.[56]

If the Iowa pattern is typical of many states, it would appear that, particularly in one-party states, the state supreme courts may be gradually fulfilling a role similar to that of the Canadian Senate—that of a haven of refuge for superannuated political leaders of secondary rank. Yet Iowa's judiciary manifested all of the attributes of institutionalization which, in terms of Huntington's thesis, pur-

[54] Rodney F. Mott, "Judicial Influence," *30 American Political Science Review* (1936), pp. 295–315.

[55] Thomas A. Ewers, *A Study of the Backgrounds of the Successful and Unsuccessful Candidates for the Iowa Supreme Court* (Iowa City: unpublished M.A. thesis, Department of History, 1959), and John W. Wood, *A Study of the Iowa Judiciary* (Iowa City: unpublished doctoral dissertation, Department of Political Science, 1956).

[56] For the data upon which these conclusions are based see John R. Schmidhauser, "Polsby Revisited: Does 'Institutionalization' Enhance Power and Influence?" a paper delivered to the Conference on the Concepts and Methods of Comparative Legislative Study, Quail Roost Conference Center, Rougemont, North Carolina, February 25–27, 1970; revised for publication in Allan Kornberg (ed.), *Legislatures in Comparative Perspective* (New York: David McKay, scheduled for 1971).

portedly enhances influence in the political and social system. Even if, as Hurst argued, the federal and state judiciaries were the beneficiaries of the relative decline of the influence and prestige of the legislatures, it should be recognized that in a broader sense all public institutions may have suffered a relative loss of prestige and influence to private institutions such as the emergent corporate law firms and major nationwide corporations so influential upon public policy after the Civil War.

A preliminary investigation of biographical sources for the members of the U.S. Supreme Court highlights the subtle transition. It is probable that the Supreme Court of the United States was the institution least likely to be affected by the changes in institutional attitudes. But pressures on the justices were quite visible in the middle and late 19th century, the period identified by Hurst as one of a relative decline of the legislature's influence and prestige. A President who strongly desired a firm ideological representative of his political party on the Supreme Court preferred an individual who would serve as long a time as possible. Thus Thomas Jefferson nominated 32-year-old William Johnson (1804–1834), hoping for strong anti-Federalist cooperation from the Bench. President Millard Fillmore, a Whig, provided a candid description in his letter to Secretary of State Daniel Webster just prior to the nomination of 41-year-old Benjamin Curtis (1851–1857):

> . . . The vacancy occasioned by the death of Judge Woodbury will soon have to be filled, . . . I believe that Judge McLean is the only Whig now upon the bench. . . . I am therefore desirous of obtaining as long a lease, and as much moral and judicial power as possible, from this appointment. I would therefore like to combine a vigorous constitution with high moral and intellectual qualifications, a good judicial mind, and such age as gives a prospect of long service. . . .[57]

Peter Vivian Daniel was appointed by President Andrew Jackson to a federal district judgeship for the eastern district of Virginia in 1836, where he served until his appointment to the U.S. Supreme Court in 1841. Daniel's biographer, John P. Frank, gave a revealing insight into the realities confronting federal judicial officials in this era, especially their relationship with Congress. He pointed out that

[57] Benjamin R. Curtis, *The Life and Writings of Benjamin Robbins Curtis* (Boston: Little, Brown and Company, 1879), p. 155.

. . . these were most unhappy years for Daniel. His judicial salary of $1800 a year was wholly inadequate for his support. His normal income prior to this appointment must have been approximately double that figure. Moreover revenue from the farm undoubtedly fell materially with the depression of 1837. He had accepted the position with the confident hope that its pay would be increased, and he was intently concerned with the prospect of such legislation during much of his district court service.

Peter and Lucy practiced strict economy, but they had scarcely been living lavishly even before he took the new position, and economy very rapidly approached hardship. Within the first year of his judicial service Daniel gave up his carriage and even his riding horse. True, Richmond was a small town and he could get about by foot, but in addition to making his situation embarrassingly evident, the new transportation arrangement made it awkward to get to the farm. With three children to educate, and with a white house servant costing $150 a year in pay, the Daniels began to run into debt at a rate of about $700 a year.

In these circumstances, Daniel began to think seriously of returning to his law practice. His practice had never been rich, but the approaching end of the careers of three of the lawyers of the city gave him new prospects, and his irritation at withdrawing from social life for reasons of economy was some incentive to give up the judicial position.

In this period the salaries of the various Federal district judges were not uniform but varied from district to district. They were set by special legislation and were determined by the amount of work thought to be involved. Senator Rives proposed an increase for Daniel's district, and the House Judiciary Committee reported a bill in 1838 to raise the salaries in seven districts to amounts ranging from $1500 for New Hampshire to $3000 for the eastern district of Pennsylvania. The salary in Daniel's district was to be set at $2500.

Daniel kept the mails full pushing this legislation. He sent several letters to President Van Buren encouraging him to support the bill, and he kept in close touch with Rives. He blasted the whole system of paying judges "like day laborers by the quantum rather than for the quality of what they are to perform," which he said was "grossly absurd." He puffed the amount of his labors a little to Rives, claiming that he was on the bench for ten weeks out of the year and was subject to call in his chambers for various orders at other times; and in a burst of vainglory he told Van Buren about the fine income he would have were he to return to his practice and about the more lucrative positions he might have taken if he had not accepted the district judgeship on the assumption that it was to be put upon a proper salary.[58]

Most striking was the experience of Justice Benjamin P. Curtis who, unlike Daniels and Clifford, did not fulfill the hopes of his political supporters by remaining on the Court as long as possible. Curtis' letter to George Tichnor put the matter as follows:

> Before [September] I shall have to come to a decision upon a matter of great moment to myself,—whether to continue to hold my present office. The expenses of living have so largely increased, that I do not find it practicable to live on my salary, even now; and, as my younger children will soon call for much increased expenses of education, I shall soon find it difficult to meet expenses by my entire income. Indeed I do not think I can do so without changing, in important particulars, my mode of life. Added to this, I cannot have a house in Washington, and I must either live apart from my family for four to six months every year while I go there, or subject them to a kind of migrant life in boarding-houses, neither congenial or useful. I had hoped it would prove otherwise, and looked forward to being able to have a house there for six months in a year. But what with the increase of luxury and the greatly enhanced prices there, I have now no hope of being able to do this. I can add something to my means by making books, but at the expense of all my vacations, when perhaps I ought not to labor hard. The constant labor of the summer has told on my health during the last two years. Such is the actual state of the case as respects my duty to my family. Then as regards the court and the public, I say to you *in confidence*, that I can not feel that confidence in the court, and that willingness to cooperate with them, which are essential to the satisfactory discharge of my duties as a member of that body; and I do not expect its condition to be improved. On the other hand, I suppose there is a pretty large number of conservative people in the Northern, and some of the Southern States, who would esteem my retirement a public loss, and who would think that I had disappointed reasonable expectations in ceasing to hold the office; and particularly in my own circuit I believe my retirement would be felt to be a loss which would not presently be fully supplied. But I do not myself think it of great public importance that I should remain where I believe I can exercise little beneficial influence and I think all might abstain from blaming me when they remember that I have devoted

[58] John P. Frank, *Justice Daniel Dissenting: A Biography of Peter V. Daniel, 1784–1860* (Cambridge, Mass.: Harvard University Press, 1964), pp. 247–248.

> six of the best years of my life to the public service, at great pecuniary loss, which the interest of my family will not permit me longer to incur. I have no right to blame the public for not being willing to pay a larger salary; but they have no right to blame me for declining it on account of its inadequacy.[59]

Justice Samuel Freeman Miller's judicial tenure (1862–1890) spanned what may well have been a crucial period in the institutional transitions noted in this preliminary investigation. He remained a steadfast advocate of an older, simpler tradition in American politics and law. His excellent biographer Charles Fairman described the era's characteristic of private corporate institutional expansion at the expense of public institutional prestige in his final chapter on Justice Miller:

> In a day when public virtue was no commonplace, Miller remained poor, honest, unwarped in sympathy or intellect. He lived well as befitted his office, but his personal tastes were of the simplest. Congress, he felt, was generous in compensating the justices at $6000, presently $10,000, per annum. In this he was speaking for himself. For when he had lost Judge Dillon as a colleague on the circuit, and then Judge McCrary, both of whom became counsel to railroad companies, he expressed his regret "that by a niggardly policy and insufficient salaries, the best offices of the country, especially its judicial offices, are abandoned for the pursuits of private life." One Sunday morning Roscoe Conkling called by appointment on Judge Miller. At lunch the latter remarked that Conkling had brought him offers of four retainers at $25,000 each, to act as consulting attorney for certain New York firms, the employment leaving him free to represent any other interest not competing with his clients. The question instantly was, "Well, what did you say?" Mrs. Miller would have been well content to have so much larger an income. Miller's reply was that he had told Conkling that he supposed he must still be worth $10,000 to the government. He would not consent to Mrs. Miller's investing in property along Sixteenth Street lest it appreciate greatly and he be accused of speculation. Whatever he had in his purse was available to all who had claims upon him.[60]

The wealth of biographical material on the justices of the U.S. Supreme Court now is being complemented by studies of the members

[59] Curtis, *op. cit.*, pp. 247–248.

[60] Charles Fairman, *Mr. Justice Miller and The Supreme Court, 1862–1890* (Cambridge, Massachusetts: Harvard University Press, 1939), pp. 426–427.

of the highest appellate courts of the states. Indicative of the kind of evidence that supports the Iowa findings in other state jurisdictions is the initial evidence from material relating to New Hampshire. For example, Roscoe Pound described Chief Justice Charles Doe of the Supreme Court of New Hampshire as the "one judge upon the bench of a state court who stands out as a builder of law since the Civil War." Yet the state historian of New Hampshire did not include Doe among the state's distinguished jurists and judges, although he did include the general counsel for the Illinois Central Railroad.[61] During the very period in which Chief Justice Doe achieved his greatest judicial contributions, he worked under very limiting conditions. His biographer described the circumstances of a major antimonopoly suit as follows:

> Doe agreed to hold a hearing in Concord the following week. Since the United States Circuit Judge was using the Mayor's office, where the court usually met, the hearing was conducted in Mitchell's law office—an illustration of the adverse physical conditions under which Doe worked: he not only lacked law clerks and secretarial help, but he did not always have chambers in the state capitol.[62]

LEGISLATIVE AND JUDICIAL CAREER PATTERNS

Nelson Polsby focused upon the political career patterns of the Speakers of the House to trace the development of institutional autonomy and the growth of internal complexity. During the 19th century, the Speakership was a political office regarded as interchangeable with political posts outside the institutional framework of the House of Representatives. Thus, after serving in the Speakership, holders of that office pursued political career goals as different as the Presidency of the United States and the mayorality of Auburn, New York and as diverse as the tax collectorship of Tappahanock, Virginia, or the lieutenant-governorship of Kentucky.[63] As a political institution, the U.S. House of Representatives (by this measure) bore a greater similarity to the highest court of Iowa than to its national

[61] John Phillip Reid, *Chief Justice: The Judicial World of Charles Doe* (Cambridge, Massachusetts: Harvard University Press, 1967), pp. 434–435.

[62] *Ibid.*, p. 368.

[63] Polsby, *op. cit.*, pp. 148–152.

judicial counterpart, the Supreme Court of the United States. Through much of the 19th century and portions of the 20th century, Iowa Supreme Court members often moved from the highest state appellate court to other political posts; thus a George Wright became a U.S. Senator, or a Joseph Reed went to the U.S. House of Representatives.[64]

It is significant that through much of its history the U.S. Supreme Court apparently possessed more of the attributes of institutional autonomy than most of its counterparts in the states. Further, it surpassed the U.S. House and Senate in these attributes. What characteristics of the U.S. Supreme Court have contributed to its institutional distinctiveness? Although available data is not strictly comparable, the significance of tenure on good behavior for the Supreme Court justices in contrast to the instability of tenure which characterizes the legislative and the other judicial systems should not be underestimated. But the influence of professional and institutional socialization is worthy of serious evaluation. Everett Hughes once argued that one of the differences between lay and professional thinking concerning work is that to the layman the technique of the occupation is merely a means to an end, while to the professional the occupation becomes an art. Hughes' perceptive distinction may contribute a great deal to understanding the unique institutional attitudes that members of the Supreme Court have developed with respect to the key question in the life cycle of every public office holder—when and why should service in a particular political institution be terminated?

The higher appellate judge is a professional among professionals.[65] His work may attain distinctive literary as well as legal excellence, as the work of a Holmes or a Cardozo attests. In terms of what Karl Llewellyn called the craft tradition of higher appellate judging, when and under what circumstances do justices of the Supreme Court leave the bench voluntarily? Voluntary separation from judicial service means those steps to terminate judicial service that are discretionary, such as retirement or resignation, as distinguished from those such as death or serious illness that may compel separation from judicial service.

[64] Schmidhauser, "Polsby Revisited," *op. cit.*

[65] Considerable portions of my exploratory study "When and Why Justices Leave the Supreme Court" in Donahue and Tibbitts, *op. cit.*, pp. 117–131, has been revised and utilized herein. The typology of justices has been expanded to include recent changes in the composition of the Supreme Court.

In many occupations of a nonprofessional kind, selection and termination of service-age patterns are determined in such a manner that individual expectations are subordinated to general institutional requirements. The biographies of the 98 individuals who have served on the Supreme Court indicate clearly that the nature of the institution, its demands on its personnel, and its position in the American political system create unique conditions influencing the individual justice's decision to voluntarily terminate his services. We may utilize the rich biographical source material on the justices to answer several questions: At what stage in his career does the truly able higher appellate judge experience a sense of fulfillment with respect to his work on the bench? What about his less able colleagues? Do the mediocre justices cling more or less tenaciously to their posts? Do factors other than a sense of institutional fulfillment mitigate against personal decisions to leave the bench before the ravages of age adversely affect the judicial product? Does the political party variable, which figures so prominently in modern studies of nonjudicial political behavior, influence decisions to terminate service on the Supreme Court? Do other factors, such as the intensity of lifelong ideological attachments, impel the able as well as the mediocre appellate judges to remain on the Supreme Court as long as possible? The academic tendency to concentrate upon judicial voting has often caused scholars to overlook other measurable aspects of the behavior of justices. What aspects of their political socialization may shed light upon their behavior in this regard?

POLITICAL SOCIALIZATION OF JUDGES

The men who eventually achieved a seat on the U.S. Supreme Court or the Federal Courts of Appeal have generally been chosen from families which were economically comfortable, politically active, ethnically "acceptable," and socially of high status. Although the United States has never evolved a political aristocracy comparable to Namier's "inevitable Parliament men," it has developed, in state and local politics, families with a long and successful heritage of political involvement. A rather high percentage of the justices came from such families. In addition, fully a third of them came from families having a long tradition of judicial service on the highest state appellate courts or the federal courts. The biographies underscore the fact that out of such family settings developed a high sense of political expectation and a political style which denoted familiarity with the political realities. For many of the potential justices it encompassed more than the twin facets of political socialization, ideological and party orientation and ordinary participation; rather it served to generate a veritable sense of political destiny.

The education of the justices also sharpened their ideological awareness and broadened the scope of their political contacts. This was perhaps even more true of those who received their law training from private tutors than of those trained in the more select law schools, for the tutors were usually the leading practitioners in the community or the state and were ordinarily among the top political leaders in the contemporary scene. In virtually every case, the private tutor later served as a political sponsor for his former pupil. Unlike most European judges, the American higher appellate judge usually did not pursue a career as a judge through his early adult years. Legislative and executive office-holding and an occasional stint in top political-party management were virtually inevitable steps in his career. Men who spent their entire adult lives as judges, such as Learned and Augustus Hand, are perhaps as rare on the Courts of Appeals as a Holmes, a Cardozo, or a Gray is on the Supreme Court of the United States. Because a rather full political career usually precedes attainment of a higher appellate judgeship, it is apt to be in his middle years—his forties or early fifties—that the prospective candidate achieves such a judicial office.

By the time such individuals attained the appellate bench, they were, in effect, polar opposites of the elderly members of McLain's California Institute of Social Welfare movement. As Frank Pinner and his associates have cogently pointed out, McLain's group of oldsters comprises many who in their advanced years show strong evidence of status-anxiety. Those rather deeply involved in achieving their organization's objectives express a strong sense of alienation from the community.[66] In contrast, the higher appellate judges, and in particular the justices of the Supreme Court, have participated in the mainstream of political and social events in their states and the nation in the years before they were selected as appellate judges. The strong sense of political efficacy engendered by political family background, educational experiences, and a full and usually successful

[66] Frank A. Pinner, Paul Jacobs, and Philip Selznick, *Old Age and Political Behavior: A Case Study* (Berkeley: University of California Press, 1959).

political career in early and middle adult life tends to remain strong after a seat on a higher appellate court is achieved.

In sum, most individuals who secure a high appellate court judgeship have a very keen awareness of the political and ideological significance of the post, possess a highly developed sense of their political efficacy, and are rarely impelled by economic circumstances to consider leaving the bench for a more lucrative post.

A TYPOLOGY OF RESPONSES TO THE JUDICIAL ENVIRONMENT

Despite the fact that virtually all the higher appellate judges and Supreme Court justices came to the bench with an acute sense of the ideological and political significance of their judicial office, several fairly distinct categories of individual adjustment to the judicial way of life may be discerned.

The Malcontents

For a tiny minority of members of the U.S. Supreme Court, the judicial mode proved to be too confining or too unrelated to the contemporary problems they deemed most challenging. Thus David Davis willingly gave up his associate justiceship for a seat in the Senate, Charles Evans Hughes resigned to seek the Presidency, and John H. Clarke resigned in 1922 to devote the remainder of what proved to be a long life to fight for American participation in the League of Nations.[67] All left the Supreme Court in the prime of life (Hughes was later made Chief Justice). A few other justices, notably John McLean and Salmon P. Chase, would have joyously left the bench for coveted Presidential nominations, but when the lightning failed to strike, they remained on the Supreme Court until their deaths.

It is noteworthy that only one of the 98 justices resigned while in full vigor in order to enjoy a life of leisure. Justice Shiras, the only justice who reached the bench without a fairly intensive political

[67] See Willard L. King, *Lincoln's Manager: David Davis* (Cambridge: Harvard University Press, 1960); Merlo J. Pusey, *Charles Evans Hughes* (New York: Macmillan Company, 1951), and Charles Wittke, "Mr. Justice Clarke: A Supreme Court Judge in Retirement," *36 Mississippi Valley Historical Review* (1950), pp. 27–50.

career, resigned in robust health at age 71. He withdrew to a comfortable retirement—wintering in Florida and summering in Michigan, with occasional stops at his native Pittsburgh.[68] Thus, aside from Shiras and a handful of justices who found the Court too confining, most members of the Supreme Court were impelled by a strong sense of the ideological importance of their position to remain in active service as long as possible.

The justices are susceptible to the same infirmities that others experience with advancing years. The full treatment of this aspect of judicial life by Charles Fairman[69] scarcely needs restatement here. Suffice it to say that in spite of the ravages of age, many judges doggedly remained on active duty because they were determined to fulfill a particular ideological mission. When several of the infirm happened to be serving on the Court simultaneously, the Supreme Court's business suffered correspondingly. Willard King pointed to one such situation during the last years of Chief Justice Fuller. In the 1909 term (October 1909 to May 1910) Moody was incapacitated, Peckham died in October, Brewer died in March, and Fuller himself bordered on senility. When Fuller died later in 1910, Holmes wrote, "The Chief died at just the right moment, for during the last term he had begun to show his age in his administrative work. . . ."[70]

For most justices who remained on the Supreme Court in their declining years, the most striking manifestation of age was a sharp decline in the number of opinions written in each successive year. But opinion-writing is not, of course, the only ingredient of Court work. Many justices exercised powerful influence despite the infirmities of age and a subsequent lessening of opinion-writing. The extent of their influence turned largely upon individual responses to the judicial environment.

The Dogged Failures

Periodically, men appointed to the Supreme Court have been mediocre justices, lacking the temperament and capacity to write well-reasoned opinions and to meet the intellectual challenges and pace of the conference. Philip Greeley Clifford wrote of his grandfather, Justice Nathan Clifford, as follows:

[68] William W. Shiras, *Justice George Shiras, Jr., of Pittsburgh* (Pittsburgh: University of Pittsburgh Press, 1953).

[69] Fairman, "The Retirement of Federal Judges," *op. cit.*, pp. 397–443.

[70] King, *op. cit.*, pp. 309–310.

> Nathan was not brilliant. . . . He possessed the ability for hard work and the slow, plodding, retentive mind. . . . The tasks before him had to be done, and were faithfully and laboriously accomplished without apparent thought of anything else.[71]

Justice Clifford, the last appointee of President Buchanan, was determined to remain on the Court until a Democratic President could replace him. He almost made it but died just a few years before Grover Cleveland's election in 1884. Justice Samuel Freeman Miller's letter opposing the reappointment of former Justice John Archibald Campbell described Clifford's condition.

> In the name of God what do I and Waite and Field, all men in our sixty-first year, want with another old, old man on the Bench? Pascal[']s *Constitution* makes Campbell seventy-five some time this year, and Judge Clifford thinks that when they served together they were about the same age and he is near seventy-four. Campbell looks five years older. I have already told the Attorney General that if an old man is appointed we should have within five years a majority of old imbeciles on the bench, for in the hard work we have to do no man ought to be there after he is seventy. But they will not resign. Neither Swayne nor Clifford whose mental failure is obvious to all the Court, who have come to do nothing but write garrulous opinions and clamor for more of that work have any thought of resigning.[72]

Obsession with real or imagined inadequacy on the bench apparently never impelled a justice to resign. However, such anxiety purportedly eventuated in the suicide of Judge W. Lynn Parkinson of the 7th Circuit Appeals Court in October, 1959.[73] The discernible effect of a sense of inadequacy among the justices was abrupt withdrawal from extrajudicial social affairs. Matthew McDevitt's appraisal of Justice McKenna provided a remarkable example of the kind of psychological response which could have far-reaching consequences for the sensitive small-group relationship basic to the internal operation of the Court. McDevitt, who incidentally was a "friendly" biographer, wrote that

[71] Phillip Greeley Clifford, *Nathan Clifford, Democrat* (New York: G. Putnam's Sons, 1922), pp. 5, 331.

[72] Fairman, *Mr. Justice Miller*, *op. cit.*, p. 351.

[73] Charles Nicodemus, "He Feared Court Job Was Out of His League," *Chicago Daily News*, November 6, 1959, Section B, p. 1.

> [McKenna was] regarded as somewhat slow in his mental processes, confused in his logic and lacking in easily definable legal philosophy. . . . During his twenty-seven years on the bench Justice McKenna led a secluded and retired life. Although invited to numerous social functions he refused to accept lest he be deprived of the time which he believed should be devoted to his heavy court duties. He could invariably be found at his desk in his study from eight o'clock in the morning and after dinner in the evening, until in his later years, when poor eyesight compelled him to forgo night work. . . . He bestowed the same care and industry on the insignificant as on controversies of pivotal import.
>
> In his early years on the bench, he [McKenna] was frequently irritable, nervous and rather unhappy because he was not familiar with the law nor *able to construct an opinion that would adequately express the convictions of his colleagues*. . . . McKenna cautiously felt his way and although his ideas were strong and forceful, yet he rarely struck out on an original line of thought. He anchored his deductions on authority and filled the pages of his opinions with numerous references and a monotonous series of diffuse and uncritical quotations. With passing years, he became more certain of his ability, and his expressions were characterized by greater breadth and independence of thought. *He became increasingly assertive of his own views until his self-assuredness almost amounted to impatience with the conclusions of others.*[74]

In short, the mediocre justice tended to keep his place on the court with as much tenacity and often with as great a sense of ideological mission as his abler colleagues.

The Competent Justices

By and large most members of the Supreme Court were neither mediocre nor great. Rather they were persons of more than average ability and legal competence who fulfilled their judicial responsibilities with vigor and competence. Their responses to the ravages of age turned largely on the prospects for the political and ideological causes to which, through a lifetime of political combat, they were committed. Those who reached an advanced age convinced that the President

[74] Italics mine; Matthew McDevitt, *Joseph McKenna, Associate Justice of the United States* (Washington: Catholic University Press, 1946), pp. 202–203, 225–226. For an incisive analysis of McKenna's retirement, see Walter F. Murphy, "In His Own Image: Mr. Chief Justice Taft and Supreme Court Appointments," *1961 Supreme Court Review*, pp. 159–193.

would appoint an ideologically sound successor were usually content to resign or retire. Gabriel Duval, for example, though deaf and rather feeble, refused to resign until assured by the Court's Clerk that Taney would be nominated to replace him.

Those justices who feared that the President would nominate ideologically unsuitable persons usually sought to remain on the court until a more acceptable appointing authority appeared on the scene. It is interesting to compare the views on senility of Taft as President and later as Chief Justice.

President Taft wrote in the following manner to Circuit Judge [later Justice] Horace Lurton:

> The condition of the Supreme Court is pitiable, and yet those old fools hold on with a tenacity that is most discouraging. Really the Chief Justice [Fuller, then 76] is almost senile; Harlan does no work; Brewer [72] is so deaf that he cannot hear and has got beyond the point of commonest accuracy in writing his opinions; Brewer and Harlan sleep almost through all the arguments. I don't know what can be done. It is most discouraging to the active men on the bench.[75]

Chief Justice Taft, aged and ill, had quite a different view in 1929. He confided to his brother Henry as follows:

> I am older and slower and less acute and more confused. However, as long as things continue as they are, and I am able to answer in my place, I must stay on the court in order to prevent the Bolsheviki from getting control . . . the only hope we have of keeping a consistent declaration of constitutional law is for us to live as long as we can. . . . The truth is that Hoover is a Progressive just as Stone is, and just as Brandeis is and just as Holmes is.[76]

The thwarting of the political hopes or ambitions of even the most restless of the relatively competent justices did not usually result in an early resignation, for strong ideological conviction usually made them determined to stay on the Court untii the political tides turned. There were, of course, a few exceptions. Interestingly enough, university teaching emerges as the alternative toward which some of the more disheartened justices occasionally turned. For example, Joseph Story had for some years expressed a determination to stay on the Court in the hope that the Whigs would be in a position to replace

[75] Henry F. Pringle, *The Life and Times of William Howard Taft* (New York: Farrar and Rinehart, Inc., 1939), pp. 529–530.
[76] *Ibid.*, p. 967.

him. Near the close of his career, he felt despondent about the prospects of another Whig Presidential victory. Further, he became convinced that conservative influence could be best developed in the "better" schools. Shortly before his death, he actually planned to resign from the Supreme Court to devote full time to his teaching post at Harvard. His underlying confidence in the long-range effectiveness of indoctrination in the schools was summed up on one occasion after a particularly tart criticism of Democratic President Van Buren's sub-Treasury plan. Story wrote:

> I think, however, the better men are acquiring a higher tone of thinking. *We talk the matter into our law students daily.* They begin already to be wide awake to the dignity of the law and its morals.[77]

William Howard Taft had long desired an appointment to the Supreme Court, but during the Wilson years he despaired. He chose as the next most important vehicle for the promotion of conservative ideas a university teaching post. Taft was pleased to teach constitutional law at Yale Law School until Harding's victory set the stage for his later appointment to the Chief Justiceship. Writing on his acceptance of the professorship, Taft said:

> I feel there has been a good deal of erroneous doctrine taught in our universities and that young men go out without having the proper sense of proportion as to the actualities of life, and especially their political and economic concepts need revision. If I can do anything to help this along, it will be full satisfaction to me, for there is nothing in life quite equal to the thought of being useful. [He desired to] keep the heterodox and wild notions that are prompted by some professors of political economy [out of the heads of the men of Yale]. I think I shall be doing God's service.[78]

For most of the competent justices, ideological fulfillment or the hope of such fulfillment could be achieved by remaining on the Court as long as possible.

The Great Justices

The criteria for greatness have been determined in part by the special demands of the Supreme Court as a political institution. Political

[77] Italics mine; William W. Story (ed.), *The Life and Letters of Joseph Story* (Boston: Charles C. Little and James Brown, 1851).

[78] Pringle, *op. cit.*, pp. 850–851.

sagacity (by eulogists termed "judicial statesmanship"), high intellectual ability, and usually a keen sense of literary creativity comprise the key ingredients. Marshall, William Johnson, Taney, Curtis, Campbell, Miller, Field, Bradley, Holmes, Hughes, Stone, Brandeis, and Cardozo clearly demonstrated these qualities. What was the nature of their responses to the problems created by advancing years? Except for Curtis and Campbell, all remained on the Court either until their deaths or until failing health necessitated resignation or retirement. Campbell joined the Confederacy, while Curtis decided to abandon the bench for a combination of ideological and economic reasons, as Curtis' previously cited letter to Tichnor indicated.

Curtis' letter presents a very revealing account of the status of the justices in mid-19th-century America. Most justices were so strongly motivated with respect to the ideological significance of their post that they willingly remained on the bench despite its obvious burdens.

Some of the more influential justices, like Field, remained on the Court long enough to experience the sweet sense of ideological victory. Others, like Miller, felt a deep sense of ideological defeat and hopelessness. Despite the following strong expression of despair, Miller remained on the bench until his death.

> I confess that much as I like the law as a science, its practice as a pursuit, and the office of Judge as filling my ambition, I find its monotony begins to pall upon my taste and feelings.
>
> I have for thirteen years given all my energies and my intellect to the duties of my office, and to the effort to make and to keep our court what it should be. If I had been made Chief Justice I think I should never have tired in this effort. And I may be more affected by the fact that I was not than I am conscious of.
>
> But I certainly strove very hard last term to have things go right and to get all the good out of our Chief and my brethren that could be had.
>
> But I feel like taking it easy now. I can't make a silk purse out of a sow's ear. I can't make a great Chief Justice out of a small man. I can't make Clifford and Swayne, who are too old, resign, nor keep the Chief Justice from giving them cases to write opinions in which their garrulity is often mixed with mischief. I can't hinder Davis from governing every act of his life by his hope of the Presidency, though I admit him to be as honest a man as I ever knew. But the best of us cannot prevent ardent wishes from coloring and warping our inner judgment.
>
> It is vain to contend with judges who have been at the bar the advocates for forty years of railroad companies, and all the forms of as-

sociated capital, when they are called upon to decide cases where such interests are in contest. All their training, all their feelings are from the start in favor of those who need no such influence.

I am losing interest in these matters. I will do my duty but will *fight* no more. I am perhaps beginning to experience that loss of interest in many things which is the natural result of years, and which wise men have felt the necessity of guarding against as age approaches.[79]

It is noteworthy that this letter was written on December 5, 1875, over 15 years before Miller's career on the Court was terminated by death. The remainder of his career scarcely bore out this prediction of diminishing vigor and interest. Miller was a strong influence throughout his tenure.

One of the most striking illustrations of the force of deep ideological conviction tempered strongly by a powerful sense of institutional responsibility was provided by Chief Justice Roger B. Taney. In his private correspondence, Taney exhibited strong sympathy for the position of the South in the rapidly intensified slavery controversy that preceded the Civil War. He hoped to name as his successor Justice John Archibald Campbell, an Alabaman of the Calhoun wing of the Jacksonian Democratic party.[80] Conversely, Taney's voting record and his case-assignment policies indicated that he sought to find "middle ground" doctrinally to preserve the integrity of the institution over which he presided.

Because of the importance he attached to his work on the Court, Taney by sheer will power and careful utilization of his waning physical resources remained on the court until 1864. Curtis provided the following portrait of Taney as he appeared when Curtis came to the Court in the middle 1850s:

He [Taney] was . . . seventy-three years old. . . . I observe that it has been recently said, by one who had known him upwards of forty years, that during all those years there had never been a time when his death might not reasonably have been anticipated within the next six months. Such was the impression produced on me when I first knew him. His tall, thin form, not much bent with the weight of years, but exhibiting in his carriage and motions great muscular weakness, the apparent feebleness of his vital powers,

[79] Fairman, *op. cit.*, pp. 373–374.

[80] Carl Brent Swisher, *Roger Brooke Taney*, *op. cit.*, pp. 492–493; George W. Duncan, "John Archibald Campbell," *5 Transactions of the Alabama Historical Society* (Montgomery: Brown Printing Company, 1904).

> the constant and rigid care necessary to guard what little health he had, strongly impressed casual observers with the belief that the remainder of his days must be short. But a more intimate acquaintance soon produced the conviction that his was no ordinary case, because he was no ordinary man. An accurate knowledge of his own physical condition and its necessities; an unyielding will, which, while it conformed everything to those necessities, braced and vivified the spring of life; a temper which long discipline had made calm and cheerful, and the consciousness that he occupied and continued usefully to fill a great and difficult office, whose duties were congenial to him, gave assurance, which the event has justified, that his life would be prolonged much beyond the allotted years of man. . . . His physical infirmities disqualified him from making those learned researches, the results of which other great judges have illustrated and strengthened their written opinions; but it can truly be said of him that he rarely felt the need of them. The same cause prevented him from writing so large a proportion of the opinions of the court as his eminent predecessor; and it has seemed to me probable that for this reason his real importance in the court may not have been fully appreciated, even by the Bar of his own time. For it is certainly true . . . that the surpassing ability of the Chief Justice, and all his great qualities of character and mind, were more fully and constantly exhibited in the consultation-room, while presiding over and assisting the deliberations of his brethren, than the public knew, or can ever justly appreciate.[81]

Taney's strong determination to participate in the Supreme Court's operation carried him to an unusual climax in 1864. A statement of the issues written by him while in his last illness actually governed the reasoning of the Court in *Gordon* v. *United States*, although Taney had died by the time the decision was handed down.[82]

The foregoing indicates that strong ideological and institutional considerations often mitigated against retirement and resignation from the Supreme Court, thereby accentuating the effect of tenure.

CONCLUSION

The environment in which members of the Supreme Court interact with members of Congress encompasses a variety of relationships

[81] Curtis, *op. cit.*, p. 337.

[82] David M. Silver, *Lincoln's Supreme Court* (Urbana: University of Illinois Press, 1956).

that link the two institutions. Thus lawyers, officials of legal professional organizations, and law-school faculty members comprise the "attentive constituents" of the judiciaries in a manner similar to that of V.O. Key's "middlemen" of politics.[83] During the many decades of institutional maturation and change discussed in this chapter, fundamental developments were taking place among the private political institutions most influential in legal matters in America. The fierce antagonism often directed against lawyers during the first four decades of the 19th century gradually was replaced by conditions much more advantageous to lawyers as professionals, to the development of legal professional associations, and to the enhanced influence of corporate law firms. The frontal attacks upon lawyers typified by William Sampson's "Anniversary Discourse" of 1824, were superseded by a gradual strengthening of the position of lawyers and of the common law and by the development and growth of lawyers' associations.[84] Out of this period of transition have emerged strong private and political institutions whose total impact upon the federal judicial system is still not fully understood. Indeed, the relative paucity of information concerning the interest-group and private political roles of legal professional groups substantiates Frank Sorauf's contention that these "large and powerful groups now languish as an unexplored area of political science."[85]

By 1970, the American Bar Association had emerged from nearly a century of development as the single most influential association of lawyers in the nation. The ABA was recognized as a significant intermediary in interest-group negotiations and efforts. As such the ABA has participated regularly in the "summit" conferences of the two most influential coalitions of business-oriented interest groups—the Greenbrier Conferences and the meetings of the Conference of National Organizations.[86] Chapter 5 explores some of the relation-

[83] See G. R. Boynton, Samuel Patterson, and Ronald D. Hedlund, "The Missing Links in Legislative Politics: Attentive Constituents," *31 Journal of Politics* (August, 1969), pp. 700–701, 709–715.

[84] Compare, for example, Sampson's negative "Discourse" of 1824 with Joseph Story's inaugural discourse of 1829 and the proliferation of affirmative commentaries which were presented in the 1830s, 1940s, and 1950s in Perry Miller (ed.), *The Legal Mind in America* (Garden City, New York: Doubleday and Company, Inc. 1962), pp. 119–134, 176 ff.

[85] Quoted in Dayton McKean's foreword to Donald R. Hall, *Cooperative Lobbying—The Power of Pressure* (Tuscon, Arizona: The University of Arizona Press, 1969), p. vii.

[86] Hall, *op. cit.*, pp. 32–34, 188–212.

ships of this national lawyers' association to the federal judiciary, in particular, the role played by the American Bar Association as an intermediary in President-Supreme Court relations and in Congress's relations with the federal judiciary.

5

The ABA, the Congress, and the Federal Judiciary

The contemporary controversies over the nominations of Justice Abe Fortas for the Chief Justiceship in 1968, Circuit Judge Clement Haynsworth in 1969, and Circuit Judge Harrold Carswell in 1970 have vividly highlighted the significance of external influences upon the federal judicial process. Some attributes of these external influences have been perceptively described and critically analyzed by Joel Grossman in his excellent *Lawyers and Judges: The ABA and the Politics of Judicial Selection.*[1] More recently, Richard Watson and Rondal Downing completed a comprehensive study of the mode of judicial selection commonly referred to as the "Missouri Nonpartisan Court Plan" in their book entitled *The Politics of the Bench and the Bar: Judicial Selection Under the Missouri Nonpartisan Court Plan.*[2]

More than a century ago, Alexis de Tocqueville contended that "the seat of the American aristocracy is with the judges on the bench and the lawyers at the bar. . . . the lawyers are the most powerful class in the community, and the only real counterpoise to the influence of the democracy." Whereupon a contemporary American reviewer opened a long-lasting argument about that assertion. Commenting in *The United States Magazine and Democratic Review* of

[1] New York: John Wiley and Sons, Inc., 1965.
[2] New York: John Wiley and Sons, Inc., 1969.

July, 1838, De Tocqueville's critic retorted, "The members of the legal profession in this country are not the aristocracy but the agents . . . of the aristocracy . . . [which] is constituted by the owners of *accumulated* wealth, and chiefly by the moneyed men of the great commercial cities."[3] Unfortunately, much of the debate over the past 120 years merited the same sort of comment as that provided by Herbert Jacob when he said that "the debate over judicial selection continues in a 'factual vacuum.'" With respect to the social and political roles of legal professionals in Missouri, Watson and Downing provided a refreshing departure by gathering empirical evidence derived from the lawyer populations of St. Louis and Kansas City. Their evidence provided support for de Tocqueville's critic, indicating that,

> Attorneys want certain kinds of judges on the bench who will interpret rules in a particular way because such matters affect their individual law practices. . . . In judicial selection, as in the handling of legal affairs generally, attorneys act as spokesmen of the social and economic interests they represent.[4]

Ironically, the impact of the growth of legal professionalism nationally still awaits full-scale scholarly investigation. When Deputy Attorney General Kleindienst announced that the Nixon Administration had delegated to the American Bar Association a veto power over all federal judgeships except Supreme Court appointments, he was, perhaps unintentionally, recording a landmark in the growth of private influence in the selection of federal judges. As *Washington Post* judicial reporter John P. MacKenzie put it, Kleindienst's statement to the 92nd Annual Convention of the American Bar Association "signified an extraordinary delegation of executive constitutional power to one segment of the population."[5]

Social theory buttressed by substantial empirical data has underscored the development of professional associations in 20th-century America. The modern professions possess several attributes that, in combination, have generally not been characteristic of other occupational groups. These comprise (a) the possession of (often monopoly of) specialized knowledge and skills derived from a program of organized training, (b) a commitment, whether real or ostensible,

[3] Anonymous reviewer in the *United States Magazine and Democratic Review* (July, 1938), pp. 341–49.

[4] Watson and Downing, *op. cit.*, p. 43.

[5] *Des Moines Register*, August 11, 1969, p. 1.

to service to society which transcends individual self-interest, and (c) a system governing admission to the practice or performance of these specialized duties and the disciplining of those who have been so admitted.[6] In order to attain these objectives, modern occupational groups seeking to maintain or attain professional status have felt it necessary to create strong organizations. Indeed in a practical sense, a strong organizational framework has become one of the hallmarks of modern professionalism. The particular significance of legal professionalism naturally relates to its claims of special competence in law-making and law interpretation. This commitment was often associated, in the historical development of the American Bar Association since 1878, with a sense of ideological mission.

In the words of the ABA's first president, James Broadhead, a legal elite must curb the excesses and errors of "public opinion" which is "so often wrong."[7] The concept that the bar must fulfill this special role is referred to again and again in internal ABA discussions, whether in Andrew Allison's quaint but perceptive reference to the "inner Republic, formed of Bench and Bar, to whose wisdom, moderation, and patriotism" important questions affecting the status of corporations must be submitted[8] or in the hardheaded, albeit less alliterative, assertions of legal elitism made in the contemporary scene. In a word, the ABA's keen interest in uniform state laws was intimately related to its sense of professional mission. This mission has consistently embodied the belief that leading lawyers by their possession of special skills and knowledge should oversee law-making and law interpretation not only for purposes of expert draftsmanship but to insure that the legislation embodies correct ideological principles.

David Truman's seminal study of interest groups underscored specialized knowledge and access as important indices of the relative influence of such groups.[9] In an evaluation of the relative legislative significance of the ABA, the factor of specialized knowledge looms large not merely because lawyers obviously are supposed to know something about law and legislation and many legislators are lawyers,

[6] Willard Hurst, "The Professions in American Life," *13 Public Relations Journal* (August, 1957), pp. 11–16.

[7] *2 Annual Reports of the American Bar Association* (Baltimore: Lord Baltimore Press, 1879), p. 51. Hereinafter cited as *ABA Reports.*

[8] *7 ABA Reports* (1884), p. 256.

[9] David B. Truman, *The Government Process* (New York: Alfred A. Knopf, 1957), pp. 213–498.

but particularly because the ABA has usually been able to successfully harness the talents and energy of highly qualified practitioners and academicians in behalf of key public policy projects. Simeon Baldwin, the founder, was himself an academician of considerable merit. Over the years, the legal drafting projects of the ABA have enlisted the assistance of men of the caliber of Williston, Pound, Beale, and a host of others. The reasons for this are complex. Most leading practitioners and many academicians were understandably interested in both technical excellence and ideological soundness in law-making. Baldwin himself exemplifies this type of ABA leader. Second, the Association was highly successful in getting financial assistance for its law-drafting projects, usually from interest groups especially concerned with a particular subject-matter area. Consequently, such ABA projects often offered a rare opportunity for legal specialists, short of hiring out to interest groups, to pursue legal research with some hope of defraying the expenses.

Why did interest groups contribute to such projects? Why did they not undertake such drafting efforts with their own paid legal staffs? The ABA provided prestige, an aura of impartiality (firmly grounded in ideological "soundness"), and expert assistance presumably unavailable elsewhere. In addition, the ABA's own system of interlocking auxiliary associations coupled with a carefully developed system of cooperation with "like-minded" groups and virtually unlimited access to the seats of power, both private and public, made for a great demand for its "services." Closely related to this are subtle questions of status among leaders in the business community. Throughout the nine decades of the ABA, it has had close ties with private interest group leaders who preferred to have others do battle for them.

These factors may be seen in a close examination of the development of ABA interest-group techniques. Early in its career the ABA assumed a role as "honest broker" among interest groups while actually cementing strong ties with the corporate business community. This position became so integral a part of ABA activity that such developments were discussed fully and frankly in ABA presidential addresses and Assembly and House of Delegates (after 1937) debates and discussions. Shortly after the ABA created the National Conference of Commissioners on Uniform State Laws, ABA President James M. Woolworth took note of the fact that the assistance of the ABA was being sought out in the following manner:

> During the year, gentlemen of great respectability interested in the National Association of Credit Men have sought conferences with me, with a view to joint action of their society and ours in an effort to secure legislation looking to the suppression of fraudulent practices of insolvent debtors. . . . You may think it wise to direct the Executive Committee or the Committee on Uniform State Laws to confer with that organization with a view to united action on behalf of legislation in which it is especially concerned.[10]

Walter S. Logan's report on the work of the ABA Committee on Commercial Law indicated the degree to which the Association's committees had successfully gained access to important decision-making bodies and had reassured the business community of their ideological soundness. As Logan put it,

> We have, during the year, kept in touch with committees of both houses of Congress and with the department of the United States Attorney-General's office which has had charge of bankruptcy matters, and we have watched the course of legislation and have tried to guide it along the lines which the Association last year recommended. . . . The main thing, however, which our committee has done during the past year is to consider the question of the involuntary part of the bankruptcy law. We have thought that it should be a law not simply for the debtor, but for the creditor and the debtor; . . . (that) it should also afford some remedy by which the creditor might lay his hand upon the reckless, improvident or fraudulent debtor in time, if possible, to save part of his debt.[11]

Having early established a reputation for recommendations described as "deliberate, conservative and entirely on juridical lines,"[12] the Association soon found itself the recipient of financial contributions from other interest groups.

Occasionally, the importunings of private corporations occasioned bitter exchanges in ABA discussions. In 1905, James M. Beck was accused of preparing a report for the ABA Committee on Insurance that not only reflected the desires of major insurance companies but was written for a guaranteed fee from a major company Beck represented. This issue was never resolved, but Moorfield Storey did insist in the debate that the majority report (Beck's) "is one of the

[10] *20 ABA Reports* (1897), pp. 203–204.

[11] *23 ABA Reports* (1900), pp. 13–14.

[12] *19 ABA Reports* (1896), p. 407. This was a reference to the Reports of the Uniform Commissioners.

ablest presentations of one side of the question that has ever been put out."[13] In 1907, on the heels of the New York insurance scandals, a committee report embodying federal regulation through the postal power was defeated 110 to 78 on Beck's motion to table. The major argument against the committee report was presented by ABA member Charles E. Littlefield, who was identified as a member of the board of directors of Equitable Life Insurance Company.[14] Conflicts of this sort occurred sporadically, but they were generally resolved in accordance with the inclinations of the conservative leadership. Such resolution of these issues should have reassured the interests that maintained what was essentially a client relationship to the ABA.

Several ABA committees have had crucial influence on public policy questions for considerable time periods during the 20th century. For example, Vernon Van Dyke in his *Human Rights, the United Nations and World Community*[15] concluded that the American Bar Association's Committee on Peace and Law Through the United Nations and Senator Bricker of Ohio "were mainly responsible" for the U.S. decision during the Eisenhower Administration not to sign or ratify any U.N. covenant on human rights. Secretary of State John Foster Dulles, in 1953, not only stressed this, but, in response to the ABA and the Senate, he also announced that the United States would not sign the Convention on the Political Rights of Women adopted by the General Assembly. Dulles also indicated, in effect, that the Administration would not press for Senate approval of the Genocide Convention.

In 1967, when the Senate was considering three human-rights conventions that had been recommended in 1963 by President John F. Kennedy, the ABA committee continued its policy of strong opposition, stating that,

> When the so-called "Bricker Amendment" to limit the domestic effect of treaties in the United States was being considered, the American Bar Association was assured that it could trust the Executive Department not to sign and submit treaties ascerting the internal affairs of the United States. If such treaties as are now

[13] *28 ABA Reports* (1905), pp. 116–118.

[14] *38 ABA Reports* (1907), pp. 10–31.

[15] I am indebted to Professor Van Dyke for the opportunity to utilize his manuscript in advance of publication; see Vernon Van Dyke, *Human Rights, the United Nations and World Community* (New York: Oxford University Press, 1970), pp. 130–131.

> proposed for accession or ratification should be approved, it will become necessary to seek constitutional limitations on the treatymaking power.[16]

The 1967 actions of the ABA committee on Peace and Law Through the United Nations opposed all three Conventions proposed for ratification by President Kennedy, including the Convention on the Political Rights of Women, The Convention on Abolition of Forced Labor, and the Supplementary Convention on Slavery. But the ABA House of Delegates overruled its committee on the Slavery Convention, and the U.S. Senate subsequently endorsed that Convention. However, the ABA House of Delegates opposed the other two conventions, and its position was sustained by the U.S. Senate.[17] In 1968, the ABA committee on Peace and Law Through the United Nations was reorganized as the Committee on World Order under Law with its jurisdiction and functions redefined.

In evaluating the influence of the ABA, a twofold concept of access should be emphasized. When it moved outside its own professional concerns, the ABA cultivated those interests it sought to serve, whether for ideological or other reasons. On this front, the ABA has been consistently successful despite the passing of leaders of earlier generations who were intimates if not members of the top corporate leadership. In other words, the work of the ABA has been "in demand." A basic reason for this has been the high quality of service rendered, as exemplified by the ABA Committee on Communications report in 1932 against more governmental regulation of or competition with private radio broadcasters. The crux of the report was a rebuttal of the Newton Minnows and Nicholas Johnsons of the early 1930s.

> In 1931, the gross expenditures of American broadcasting stations reached a total of almost $78,000,000. There are 607 American broadcasting stations, all but 40 of which are privately owned and operated. The exceptions are stations directly or indirectly owned by states or municipalities. *These sums have been invested or expended to bring to American listeners without cost the most expensive, the most entertaining, the most instructive programs that human ingenuity has yet been able to devise.*[18]

[16] *Ibid.*, p. 141
[17] *Ibid.*, p. 131.
[18] Italics mine; *57 ABA Reports* (1932), p. 145.

Consistent defense of modified or complete economic freedom from governmental control or regulation was virtually the hallmark of ABA legislative and executive recommendations in domestic politics. Therefore, it was only natural that the ABA and its subdivisions would have greater access to policymakers in eras of conservative ascendance and less during periods of conservative defeat.

The impact of the great depression and the coming of the New Deal brought in its wake a suspicion of the ABA so marked that ABA leaders discussed it openly. In 1932 Paul Howland, chairman of the ABA Committee on Jurisprudence and Law Reform, was shaken by the coolness with which his committee's recommendations were received by Congressional committees. Howland complained that,

> . . . there was a feeling, not expressed, that perhaps we were not entirely welcome; at least, that possibly there was an ulterior motive back of the activities of your committee as the representative of some great corporations or wealthy clients.[19]

In 1934 the ABA Special Committee on Judicial Appointments was discontinued because, after two years of waiting, its services and advice had not once been called for by the Senate Judiciary Committee and the Justice Department.[20]

The main thrust of the ABA's programs and official positions have been ideologically conservative. The ABA opposed the Child Labor Amendment, the Wagner-Murray-Dingall (National Health Insurance) Bill, the Genocide Convention and the Covenant on Human Rights, the Ewing Health Bill, the Forand Health Bill, the Gore-Holifield Bill (providing for public development of atomic energy for peacetime purposes), and an ABA observer with the United States delegation to the United Nations. Since 1937, the ABA has vigorously supported the Bricker Amendment, the Tidelands Oil Bill, the Mundt-Nixon (Internal Security) Bill, the Reed-Dirksen Amendment (placing a 25% limit on income tax except under certain limited conditions), the Wham resolutions (in effect urging [a] Congress to guard against permitting the Supreme Court to interpret matters involving states and [b] urging transferal of many functions such as urban renewal to the states), and, during the 1950s, congressional legislation to override Supreme Court decisions involving basic procedural rights and statutory interpretations upholding

[19] *57 ABA Reports* (1932), p. 101.
[20] *59 ABA Reports* (1934), p. 261.

federal regulatory authority.[21] During the (Joseph) McCarthy era of the early 1950s the ABA put its prestige behind the investigatory thrust that dominated the period. The ABA House of Delegates adopted a strong resolution in 1952 commending the House Un-American Activities Committee and the Senate Internal Security Subcommittee on the way they conducted their hearings and investigations. During the floor action on this resolution, the ABA House of Delegates also approved an amendment submitted by Charles Rhyne to extend the ABA commendation to the McCarthy subcommittee for "conducting its inquiry in the exposition [sic] of Communist activities in a dignified, lawyerlike way, with full recognition of all the constitutional rights of those they call before them."[22]

The direct attacks upon the Supreme Court by the ABA which were the center of considerable bar controversy in 1959 have not become consistent ABA policy in the 1960s, although some prominent ABA officials have used the organization as a forum for such attacks. ABA President Satterfield of Yazoo City, Mississippi, made such a frontal assault in his presidential address in 1962.[23] By the late 1960s, attacks on the Supreme Court not only became less frequent but were sometimes replaced by positive efforts such as the ABA support for better salaries for judges and justices, a reassertion of a long-term commitment of the Association. Similarly, the ABA has, in recent years, taken affirmative positions in behalf of opportunities for legal education for potential attorneys from minority groups and has opposed the Murphy OEO Amendment. In balance, however, historically and in contemporary public-policy analyses, the official positions of the American Bar Association have frequently displayed ambivalence reflecting strong opposition to expansion of the federal government and to a larger federal regulatory role in business affairs, while concomitantly pushing for more roles for lawyers in the federal government and for higher fees. The approach was exemplified in the ABA presidential address of Sylvester C. Smith, Jr. in 1963. Smith extolled the virtues of the profession and the need for greater recognition thereof and then reasserted a

[21] John R. Schmidhauser, *The Supreme Court: Its Politics, Personalities, and Procedures* (New York: Holt, Rinehart, and Winston, 1960), pp. 77–78; see also Clifford M. Lytle, *The Warren Court and its Critics* (Tucson, Arizona: University of Arizona Press, 1968), pp. 97–101.

[22] Proceedings of the ABA House of Delegates, *38 American Bar Association Journal* (1952), p. 428.

[23] Lytle, *op. cit.*, pp. 98–99, 100.

characteristically strong denunciation of federal regulatory agencies. In Smith's terms,

> There is every indication that the federal administrative agencies are again reaching out for power, extending their jurisdiction beyond the intended delegation granted by Congress. . . . There is evidence that they have slowed down the economy of the country. If the profession is to preserve our form of government, it must dramatically bring to the attention of the members of the Congress these tendencies because they can be carried so far that the federal agencies may in the future control every phase of an individual's activities.[24]

The potential conflict between the propagation of a particular ideology, for the ABA rather consistently conservative, and the organization's claim that its public policy role is detached and impartial has become highly significant in 1969. Outgoing ABA President William T. Gossett, in presenting his final Report on the State of the ABA in August, 1969, provided a classic self-appraisal of the organization during its current period of significant influence in the Nixon Administration. As Gossett put it,

> . . . the Association continues to enjoy enormous influence and prestige among the public and private institutions of our society and among the general citizenry. Perhaps never before in its ninetieth year history have the public demands upon the Association been so formidable; and never before has it been more responsive to the needs of society and to the obligation of the profession to provide intelligent leadership.
>
> Not only does government rely increasingly upon the Association's guidance in appraising the professional qualifications of proposed appointees to judicial and other positions; heads of government agencies are making requests for counsel and advice regarding the problems of government, substantive as well as procedural. And the Association is receiving an ever-expanding number of invitations to appear before Congressional committees.
>
> *We should remind ourselves from time to time, I suggest, that the Association as an advisor of government has uncommon attributes, not only with respect to investigative and analytical competence, but in terms of basic motivation; that is, a capacity to act and speak with detachment and independence regarding the issues*

[24] Sylvester C. Smith, Jr., "Where Does the Organized Bar Go From Here?" *88 ABA Reports* (1963), p. 482.

> *involved. And its views generally have been accepted as nonpolitical and impartial.* The recently appointed commission to study the Federal Trade Commission, at the request of President Nixon, has an opportunity to add luster and credibility to the Association's *aurora popularis* as a dispassionate investigator and advocate of the public interest.
>
> Let me record in passing that not only is President Nixon a lawyer; twelve members of his cabinet and subcabinet also are members of the profession. And no fewer than fifteen of the President's appointments to key positions in federal agencies have been lawyers who have been active as officers or as Section or Committee chairmen of the Association.[25]

President Gossett's summation stressed the contention that the ABA is detached and impartial in its public policy roles. Yet its phenomenal upsurge has tended to underscore certain inherent problems such as the association's conservative ideology, in contrast to its ostensible claim to detachment, and the more important issue of who is doing the influencing—the Nixon Administration or the ABA. Only a month after publication of Gossett's message, news analysts raised several questions about the nature of the relationship. Lyle Denniston's "Washington Closeup" analysis was typical.[26] Denniston reported that

> . . . President Nixon's campaign to get many of the nation's private groups to help out on the "Nixon team" is nowhere more successful than with the American Bar Association.
>
> The big organization of the nation's lawyers is getting so close to the administration, in fact, that some of its members are quietly protesting that its independence and objectivity may suffer.
>
> The ABA has long enjoyed good relations on Capitol Hill, mainly because it was considered to be outside politics, and this lobbying advantage could suffer if the association gets too close to the White House, it has been suggested.
>
> But it is a simple fact, openly and even proudly acknowledged by some association leaders, that the ABA has "better connections" here now than in anyone's memory.
>
> Just recently, the group helped cement its relationship by agreeing to help the administration "off the hook" on the problem of campus unrest.

[25] Italics mine; See 55 *American Bar Association Journal* (August, 1969), p. 699.

[26] Lyle Denniston, "Washington Close-up," *Iowa City Press Citizen*, September 24, 1969.

Privately, key Nixon associates approached the ABA because they were concerned that Congress was about to pass strong, "anti-student" legislation—cutting off public funds to punish rebellious collegians. An ABA study could help head this off, it was said.

These officials apparently also were troubled about a study that the American Council on Education was planning into campus uprisings. The ACE was going to stage a big public conference, and the administration apparently feared that the result would not be "objective," that it would wind up too sympathetic to student grievances.

The ABA was asked to see if it could get into a joint effort with the ACE. This was done, and now a blue-ribbon commission has been set up by the ABA's new president, Philadelphia lawyer Bernard G. Segal. Once the commission has its report done, it will conduct a public conference with the ACE.

To insure that the ABA panel would have prestige, Segal named the man he succeeded as ABA president—Detroit lawyer William T. Gossett—as chairman.

Earlier this week, the ABA finished another chore which it had undertaken at the President's wish. It made a study of the operation of the Federal Trade Commission in response to a direct Nixon plea last spring.

It may be only coincidental, but the Nixon personnel recruiters have turned to the active ranks of ABA to find government executives.

A recent compilation, by the ABA itself, shows that 12 lawyers—most of them present or former heads of ABA committees—have been given significant government jobs. The list includes the top tax collector, two assistant attorneys general, the patents commissioner, the general counsels of two agencies, and the No. 2 American negotiator at the Paris talks on Vietnam.

If those appointments do represent a kind of reward to the ABA, that is hardly the whole of the administration's expression of gratitude.

More importantly, the Justice Department has promised the association that no person will be appointed to any federal judgeship (below the Supreme Court) without the advance clearance of the ABA. While Segal insists this is not "veto power," it certainly does give the private group a more certain clearance authority than it has ever had before.

Segal has promised to work for the same kind of authority over potential nominees to the Supreme Court. He has indicated that the White House or someone influential at the Justice Department has hinted that the policy of no ABA clearances for high court members may be only temporary. . . .

The suggestion that a President would allow a kind of veto power over Supreme Court nominations to a private group like the American Bar Association raises questions as serious as the delegation of such power over court of appeals and district judges. Indeed, it has been basic to the objections that students of the constitutional process have raised. The general objection is well stated by Professor Charles Black:

> I just have the feeling that no unofficial, fundamentally private body should have any special status in the process. The Constitution places the responsibility on elected officials in the Presidency and in the Senate, people who are answerable to the public for their actions, and that's where it should stay.[27]

The basic issue of whether the ABA actually maintains ideological or political neutrality and "detachment" has been raised both by critics from within the Association and by academic critics from without. One vocal critic publicly charged the ABA's leadership with tacitly accepting "flagrant abuse of the American judicial process" because it feared losing members in the South. Referring to ABA silence on the handling of the case of *Alabama* v. *Coleman*, ABA member Alfred Connor Bowman argued that the possible loss of Southern members resulting from ABA criticism of the trial would be a small price to pay to enhance the ethical authority of the Association. He also pointed out that

> Several years ago a civil rights worker was killed and his companion was wounded in Haynesville, Alabama. It is conceded by everyone concerned that the killer was a man named Coleman. Nevertheless, after a little sniggering and some obscene fun with the press, a local jury acquitted Mr. Coleman.
>
> After waiting a decent period—deemed sufficient for a ponderous national organization that had publicly charged itself with responsibility for assuring "the proper administration of justice" to speak out on this notorious, specific, abuse of the judicial process—the press began to comment on the American Bar Association's silence. A member of the official family defended total inaction on the ground that merely expressing a moral judgment would accom-

[27] Quoted in Patrick Owens, "Haynsworth and the Bar: A Jury of His Club Mates," *The Nation* (November 3, 1969), p. 464.

plish nothing. To this the national press replied generally along the lines of an editorial in the Los Angeles Times of October 27, 1965: "The point is not whether ABA statements will of themselves exercise an influence for the better. In the final analysis the point is that the ABA has an ethical and moral obligation to speak out where law is mocked and judicial processes are debased."[28]

Another area of controversy is the question of the validity or ideological direction of some aspects of research conducted by the American Bar Foundation affiliated with the ABA. It is difficult to reconcile the contention of Preble Stoltz that "The belief that there is a vast unfilled need for legal services in the middle class is nothing more than an article of faith"[29] with the academic research of the past decade. For example, Leon Mayhew and Albert J. Reiss, Jr., interviewed a sample of nearly 800 respondents in metropolitan Detroit to explore the social organization of legal contracts. They concluded that

> . . . untreated problems exist for all segments of the community. Organized to serve property and a few other problems, notably divorces and accidents, the legal profession provides relatively little professional representation and advice in relation to a broad panoply of problems surrounding such daily matters as the citizen's relation to merchants or public authority. . . .
>
> It is an interesting commentary on the legal frame of reference to note that one legal scholar has argued that such interests as rights to welfare benefits, job and retirement rights, and civil rights will only be adequately protected when lawyers come to see them as property rights.[30]

Perhaps the most serious example of ABA partiality involved the highly sensitive issues surrounding the Fortas and Haynsworth ethical issues of 1969. In the spring of 1969, the Committee on Professional Ethics of the ABA analyzed comprehensively the mean-

[28] Alfred Connor Bowman, "What Price 'Effectiveness'," *55 American Bar Association Journal* (March, 1969), pp. 251–252.

[29] Preble Stoltz, "The Legal Needs of the Public—A Survey Analysis," reported in *55 American Bar Association Journal* (July, 1969), p. 633.

[30] Leon Mayhew and Albert J. Reiss, Jr., "The Social Organization of Legal Contacts," *34 American Sociological Review* (June, 1969), p. 317. The article contains a concise reference summary of earlier research on the subject conducted and reported in the 1960s.

ing and significance of relevant canons of judicial ethics—namely Canons 1, 4, 13, 24, 25, 26, 31, 32, 33, and 34.[31]

The reinterpretation of these canons in Opinion 322 was handed down on May 18, 1969. The opinion recognized that there have been "very few opinions involving judges of courts of review." It held, however, that "it should be clear that these canons of ethics apply to judges at all levels and, probably, as they relate to appearances of impropriety, apply with greater strictness to the judges of higher courts, for the conduct of judges of higher courts sets the tone for the whole judiciary." The committee stressed that "appearances of impropriety are equally as important as improper actions themselves."

Canon 24 dealt with inconsistent obligations. It provided that a "judge should not accept inconsistent duties; nor incur obligations, pecuniary or otherwise, which will in any way interfere or appear to interfere with his devotion to the expeditious and proper administration of his official functions." Canon 32 stated that "A judge should not accept any presents or favors from litigants, or from lawyers practicing before him or from others whose interests are likely to be submitted to him for judgment."

Among the canons interpreted in Opinion 322, these had proved pertinent to the Fortas situation after the disclosures involving Louis Wolfson. But Canon 26, dealing with personal investments, was also discussed in the May, 1969, opinion. Its reappraisal was destined to have even greater significance in connection with Circuit Judge Haynsworth's nomination. Canon 26 provides that

> A judge should abstain from making personal investments in enterprises which are apt to be involved in litigation in the court; and, after his accession to the Bench, he should not retain such investments previously made, longer than a period sufficient to enable him to dispose of them without serious loss. It is desirable that he should, so far as is reasonably possible, refrain from all relations which would normally tend to arouse the suspicion that such relations warp or bias his judgment, or prevent his impartial attitude of mind in the administration of his judicial duties.
>
> He should not utilize information, coming to him in a judicial capacity, for purposes of speculation; and it detracts from the public confidence in his integrity and the soundness of his judgment for

[31] For a comprehensive listing of the relevant Canons of Judicial Ethics and the complete text of the ABA Committee Opinion (Number 322) see *55 American Bar Association Journal* (July, 1969), pp. 666–668.

him at any time to become a speculative investor upon the hazard of a margin. . . .

The ABA Committee summed up its re-evaluation of these and related canons with a strong imperative:

> The committee feels that a judge or justice should not undertake any obligations or enter into any relationship of any kind or nature whatsoever which might in any way be inconsistent with his duties and obligations as a judge or which in any way might point to impropriety on the part of a judge. . . .

The opinion of the ABA committee applied with equal insistence to the imperative of Canon 26 (relating to personal investments) and Canon 24 (relating to inconsistent obligations). In the light of this important opinion by the ABA's Committee on Professional Ethics, why did the ABA's Judiciary Committee support Judge Clement Haynsworth and why did sixteen former ABA Presidents back him? The original endorsement of Judge Haynsworth by the ABA's Judiciary Committee was made unanimously on September 5th. After several conflict-of-interest issues were raised after the September ABA endorsement, the Association's Judiciary Committee met again. This reappraisal, made on October 12, reaffirmed the committee's earlier endorsement of Haynsworth as "highly qualified." The vote was 8 to 4.[32]

Three basic issues were raised by the actions regarding Haynsworth. First, did the Association's actions show partiality by applying a standard different from that applied in the Fortas case? Second, was the ABA committee itself so constituted as to avoid conflict-of-interest charges of political import? And third, did the handling of the Haynsworth nomination reflect preferential treatment when compared to previous committee policy? These issues are all salient with respect to the basic constitutional question of whether a private group should be granted special influence in the selection of federal judges and justices.

With respect to the third question, the ABA Committee on the Federal Judiciary reported, in 1963, the following comment on Arthur Goldberg:

> As to Mr. Justice Goldberg . . . your committee reported him to be "highly acceptable from the standpoint of professional qualifica-

[32] *Washington Post* (October 13, 1969), pp. A1 & 2.

tions" having determined that it was inappropriate, in the case of a judge nominated for this particular court, to express an opinion to the degree of qualification.[33]

In contrast, the ABA Committee's two reports on Judge Clement Haynsworth *did* express an opinion on the "degree of qualification," rating him as "highly qualified." This designation represented the equivalent of at least the second highest rating on the ABA's four-point scale of evaluation. The range from lowest to highest is (4) "not qualified," (3) "qualified," (2) "well qualified," (highly?) and (1) "exceptionally well qualified."[34]

The ABA's handling of the Haynsworth matter also raised the issue of political partiality. The chairman of the ABA evaluating committee, Lawrance Walsh, served coincidentally as President Nixon's second top negotiator to the Paris Peace Conference. The ABA did not see fit to remove Walsh from his ABA committee chairmanship after his presidential appointment even though there were obvious conflict-of-interest possibilities under such conditions. Perhaps even more damaging were the repeated invocations of the ABA by President Nixon and his top officials in the closing days of the dramatic Haynsworth confirmation fight. In his last-ditch news conference in behalf of Haynsworth on October 20, 1969, President Nixon invoked the ABA on two separate occasions. Clark Mollenhoff was so confident of the ABA committee's support that he "predicted" that it would not "change its position at all" two days before the ABA committee reaffirmed its earlier finding that Haynsworth was "highly qualified" for an Associate Justiceship. In the same interview, Mollenhoff cited the ABA support as the basis for his contention that there was no similarity between the Haynsworth and Fortas situations. He argued that the ABA found that Fortas "acted 'clearly contrary' to the canons of judicial ethics" but "By contrast, the Haynsworth nomination has been supported by the ABA."[35]

Clark Mollenhoff's attempt to contrast ABA handling of the Fortas and Haynsworth cases served to highlight the issue of preferential treatment. The ABA's Opinion 322, discussed above, could have applied with equal force to both. Indeed, the *American Bar*

[33] Report of the Standing Committee on the Federal Judiciary, *88 ABA Reports* (1963), p. 195.

[34] Grossman, *op. cit.*, p. 76.

[35] *Washington Post* (October 13, 1969), p. A2.

Association Journal editorially criticized Fortas for "lack of candor" and stressed Canon 4:

> A Judge's official conduct should be free from impropriety and the appearance of impropriety . . . and his personal behavior, not only upon the bench and in the performance of judicial duties, but also in his everyday life, should be beyond reproach.[36]

But no similar criticism of Haynsworth was made despite the fact that he participated in cases involving corporations in which he owned stock, bought stock in a corporation involved in current litigation before his court, and failed to present a full account of his private business activities in his earlier appearances before the Senate Judiciary Committee. The Board of Governors and the ABA considered these issues but decided that it lacked the power and the precedents to override its Judiciary Committee by asking for an opinon of Haynsworth's conduct from its Committee on Professional Ethics.[37] In sum, the ABA's performance in connection with the Fortas and Haynsworth incidents raised anew several long-term questions about the propriety of giving Constitutionally-delegated power to a private organization. The possibility of abuse of this power is rather serious—as has been underscored in the past by the handling of the judicial candidacies of Congressman Benjamin Rabin in 1947 and that of David Rabinovitz in 1964.[38] It has become even more serious since 1969 because of the close relationship of the Nixon Administration to the ABA.

CONCLUSION

The foregoing analysis of the role of the American Bar Association suggests that the policy positions of interest groups toward the court often shift in accordance with changing circumstances and internal organizational reorientations. The ABA's close ties with the business community, its modern participation in business-oriented interest-group "summit" meetings such as Greenbrier suggest a shift to a much more critical attitude toward the Court than that taken by the ABA in the 1920s and the 1930s. Indeed such a policy shift appeared

[36] *55 American Bar Association Journal* (July, 1969), p. 648.
[37] Owens, *op. cit.*, p. 462.
[38] Schmidhauser, *op. cit.*, pp. 21–22; Owens, *op. cit.*, pp. 462–463.

to be developing throughout the 1950s and early 1960s. However, internal changes within the ABA and its multitude of subdivisions in the late 1960s and early 1970 make it rather clear that the organization does not react monolithically and that it has begun, at least in some areas, to take on a much more serious concern for nonpropertied human rights. The opposition to the Nixon Administration's preventive detention legislation by the ABA Section on Individual Rights and ABA President Bernard Segal's public criticism of Vice President Agnew's attempt to force the resignation of student James Rhodes from the President's Campus Unrest Commission[39] were contemporary manifestations of this change. In the final analysis, however, the arguments against private-group veto power over judicial appointments are compelling and serious.

[39] *Washington Post*, Friday, June 19, 1970, pp. A4, B1, and B9. The initial portions of this chapter were drawn from John R. Schmidhauser, "Legal Professionalism: Its Political Implications" (Paper delivered at the 1962 Annual Meeting of the American Political Science Association, Washington, D.C., September, 1962.)

6

The President, the Senate, and the Court: Rhetoric v. Reality

The election of a new President combined with a change in party control of the White House has always had special significance for the process of selecting members of the Supreme Court of the United States. When President-elect Richard M. Nixon took his oath of office in January, 1969, he was assured the opportunity of choosing the next Chief Justice within a span of a few months.

The greatest and most influential of the judicial appointments potentially available to an incoming President had thus fallen to Richard Nixon. This fact was especially important because the Supreme Court had once again become a storm-center of political controversy. The thrust of the 1968 presidential campaign had touched aggressively upon such themes as "permissiveness," the need for greater emphasis upon the rights of victims rather than defendants, and greater flexibility for police in the apprehension of criminals. Attacks on civil libertarian and procedural safeguards were essentially attacks on the "Warren" Court. However, the retirement of Chief Justice Warren would not necessarily bring the civil libertarian emphasis of the Supreme Court to an abrupt end. For, regardless of the characteristics of his successor to the Chief Justiceship, the remaining members of the Court were likely to continue the Warren Court tendencies, albeit by narrower voting margins. Omitting the retiring Chief Justice, six of the ten associate Justices, Black, Douglas, Brennan, White, Fortas, and Marshall, constituted with varying degrees of intensity a pro-civil-liberties majority.

Under "normal" expectations, President-elect Nixon's opportunity to change the emphasis in Supreme Court decision-making therefore was dependent upon the longevity of the Warren Court justices and their personal inclination toward retirement or resignation. In 1957 Professor Robert A. Dahl observed that "over the whole history of the Court, on the average one new justice has been appointed every twenty-two months. Thus a president can expect to appoint about two new Justices during one term in office."[1] Obviously, such an estimate has to be tempered by the circumstances of the contemporary setting—circumstances ranging from age and health to the ideological inclinations of the present members of the Supreme Court.

The two oldest members of the Warren Court, other than the Chief Justice himself, were the judicial appointees of President Franklin Delano Roosevelt—Hugo LaFayette Black, then aged 82, and William Orville Douglas, aged 70. Both were spirited judicial activists who were deeply committed on civil liberties issues, although Black has differed with Douglas on the handling of civic demonstration issues. The first Roosevelt appointee, Black left his seat in the U.S. Senate for the Supreme Court in 1937. Douglas, a Yale law professor, came to the Supreme Court in 1939 from his position as chairman of the Securities and Exchange Commission. Although a great deal of attention has currently been focused upon civil liberties cases, a tremendously important aspect of Supreme Court work centers upon domestic and international economic issues. Here the Roosevelt appointees, Black and Douglas, had been bastions of economic liberalism. And here was an area of ideological difference with the incoming Nixon Administration which presumably could have persuaded Black and Douglas to retain their places on the Bench for a few more years if health permitted.

Only one of the three Eisenhower appointees, John Marshall Harlan, approached the advanced ages of the Roosevelt appointees.

[1] Robert A. Dahl, "The Supreme Court's Role in National Policy-Making," in Sheldon Goldman and Thomas P. Jahnige (ed.), *The Federal Judicial System: Readings in Process and Behavior* (New York: Holt, Rinehart and Winston, Inc., 1968), p. 359.

Harlan, who in 1969 was 69, served for a year as a federal court of appeals judge before his Supreme Court appointment in 1955. His fellow Eisenhower appointee, William Joseph Brennan, Jr., aged 62 in 1969, and Potter Stewart, aged 53, also served as appellate judges before appointment to the Supreme Court. Brennan, a Democrat, served as a justice of the New Jersey Supreme Court before his U.S. Supreme Court appointment on the eve of the 1956 Presidential election. Stewart, like Harlan, was a Republican. He had served as a judge of the 6th Circuit Court of Appeals before elevation to the high bench in 1958.

Of the three Eisenhower appointees, Brennan had tended to vote with the Warren Court majority, while Harlan and Stewart generally had leveled the strongest judicial criticism of contemporary doctrinal trends. According to newspaper speculation in 1969, the most immediate opportunity for President-elect Nixon to fill a vacancy was alleged to be provided by Justice Harlan. Harlan's eye difficulties purportedly would make full participation in the demanding visual workload of the Supreme Court difficult. His possible retirement would not, however, have provided Nixon an opportunity to whittle down the liberal majority, because Harlan himself represented the kind of judicial conservatism likely to be sought by Nixon.

The three remaining justices were Democrats and, barring unforeseen problems of health, were considered likely to help maintain the Court's liberal tendency for some years to come. Justice Byron Raymond White, the only remaining appointee of President John F. Kennedy, came to the Court in 1962 after serving as Deputy Attorney General under the late Robert Kennedy. White, who served as a law clerk to Chief Justice Vinson during the 1946–1947 term of the Supreme Court, was in 1969 only 51. The two appointees of President Johnson were lawyers of exceptional ability. Justice Abe Fortas succeeded Arthur Goldberg in 1965. In 1969 he was 58. Justice Thurgood Marshall came to the Supreme Court from the Court of Appeals bench. He was 60 years of age, having served for many years as an exceedingly effective legal advocate for the NAACP.

This was the situation in the early weeks of the administration of President Nixon in 1969. As was indicated in Chapter 6, historically, most justices have remained on the Court through all their vigorous years and, indeed, some have remained considerably longer. Institutional custom has buttressed individual discretion by Court members regarding retirement or resignation. But the institutional traditions of the Court may be tempered by the competing thrust of other institutions. Presidential politics and Senatorial action demonstrated the continuing volatility of Court-oriented politics in the nomination controversies of Fortas, Haynsworth, and Carswell.

Of particular importance to the study of the institutional relationship of the President and the Senate regarding Supreme Court nominations is the question of whether the claimed reverence for the highest court in America manifests itself in nomination contests. The subsequent analysis of the two Fortas controversies and the nomination contests of Clement Haynsworth and Harrold Carswell provide a preliminary opportunity to determine whether or not "normal" political tactics and considerations are modified or abandoned when an issue involving judicial personnel is under consideration by the executive or legislative branches.

THE FORTAS CONTROVERSY OF 1968

The nomination of Justice Abe Fortas as Chief Justice of the United States by President Lyndon B. Johnson on June 26, 1968, stimulated a major debate in the Congress and throughout the country. The elevation of a sitting Justice to the Chief Justice's chair during a year of considerable political turmoil added much to the already heated controversy over the Warren Court, its decisions, and the issue of law and order. By elevating a member of the Supreme Court, President Johnson provided the Senate with an opportunity for a vote of confidence or no-confidence in the Warren Court. The controversy over the Court's record and its relation to the politics of the Presidential campaign quickly became key factors in the debate over the nomination. Questions involving ethics, cloture, separation of powers, and "cronyism" also were involved. However, a careful analysis of the *Congressional Record* and contemporary press commentary indicates that these issues often were not far removed—if at all—from the central issues of partisan politics and the Court's record. With the exception of several Southern senators, whose opposition was directed primarily at the Court and Chief Justice Warren, partisan considerations were paramount in spite of efforts taken by opponents of Fortas not to appear openly partisan.

The manner and circumstances surrounding Chief Justice Earl Warren's retirement and President Johnson's long-standing practice of maneuvering with high-level appointments added to the controversy. Alexander Bickel argued that most Presidents have gone to great pains not to offer such opportunities, because of the obvious boat-rocking "that must result from a direct clash between any two of the three independent and equal branches of the Federal Government."[2] Such a vote of confidence is implicit in recess appointments and "more inescapably implicit when an Associate Justice is nominated for the Chief Justiceship, and perhaps that is one reason why Chief Justices have been created by promotion from within the Court only twice before—White in 1911 and Stone in 1941."[3] Bickel's observations may be disputed with regard to degree of emphasis, but an analysis of the debates in Congress suggests that a vote of confidence or no-confidence in the Warren Court was very much a part of the Fortas controversy. In the end, senators supported and opposed Justice Fortas for a variety of reasons, but partisan opposition to the Warren Court's record was of great, if not overriding, importance.

WARREN'S RETIREMENT

Through early 1968 rumors circulated that Chief Justice Earl Warren was seriously considering retirement. Interest in the issue increased after President Johnson declared in March that he would not seek re-election. *The Wall Street Journal* on June 14, 1968, reiterated its view that Warren planned to retire in order to "have a voice in naming his successor."[4] It should be pointed out that several weeks after the content of Warren's retirement letter was made public, the Chief Justice cast considerable doubt on the credibility of the early press reports. On July 5, he held a news conference in the Supreme Court Building. In response to a direct question concerning whether he had had any discussion with President Johnson about a successor he replied, "No, I did not have."[5]

[2] Alexander M. Bickel, "Fortas, Johnson and the Senate," *New Republic* (September 28, 1968), p. 22.

[3] *Ibid.* The exact number is subject to interpretation. Alpheus T. Mason states that three justices have been promoted. See "Pyrrhic Victory: The Defeat of Abe Fortas," *The Virginia Quarterly*, Vol. 45, No. 1, Winter, 1968, p. 20.

[4] Quoted by Senator Robert Griffin, *Congressional Record*, September 18, 1968, p. S11011.

[5] U.S. Senate Committee on the Judiciary, *Hearings: Nominations of Abe Fortas and Homer Thornberry*, Part 2, September 13, 16, p. 1383.

The significance of press speculation in stimulating controversy was suggested in September, 1968, by Republican Senator Robert Griffin, the man who led the Republican opposition to Justice Fortas. The senator stated that press reports had made him aware of the issue prior to the nomination of Fortas. He went on to point out that "authoritative sources" were being quoted in newspapers as saying a letter had been received by the President with the contents remaining unknown.[6] He added that on June 22 (four days before Justice Fortas had been designated the nominee)

> before I knew anything, I indicated disagreement with the retirement and its purposes. I did not approve of the maneuver and I would oppose the nominee under the circumstances regardless whom President Johnson might name.[7]

Open opposition to President Johnson's naming the successor to Chief Justice Warren became central to the Republican plan of opposition to Fortas, with Senator Griffin leading the attack. This group, originally nineteen in number, used the "lame duck" issue in many of their statements and severely criticised the Chief Justice's manner of retirement.

After Justice Fortas had been nominated and Judge Thornberry had been nominated to assume Fortas' position on the Court, Senator Griffin and his Republican colleagues repeatedly made clear that "... the question of Mr. Fortas' or Mr. Thornberry's qualifications aren't really a part of the issue."[8] Senator Baker of Tennessee was most explicit on this point.

> I have no question concerning the legal capability of Justice Fortas, and as much as I would like to have a native Tennessean as Chief Justice, there are, in my opinion, more important considerations at this time.[9]

The issue was who would appoint Warren's successor, President Johnson or a possible Republican President and not, as was stated frequently, the manner and circumstances of Warren's resignation. The political nature of the criticism was clear in Senator Griffin's comments in July:

[6] *Congressional Record*, September 9, 1968, p. S11011.
[7] *Ibid.*, p. 11012.
[8] *Ibid.*
[9] *Congressional Record*, July 19, 1968, p. S8985.

> Never before has there been such obvious political maneuvering to create a vacancy so that the outgoing President can fill it and thereby deny the opportunity to a new President about to be elected by the people.
>
> Such maneuvering at a time when the people are in the process of choosing a new government is an affront to the electorate. It suggests a shocking lack of faith in our system and the people who make it work.
>
> It should surprise no one that such a political maneuver has been met head-on by a political response from within the Senate. Indeed, it would signal a failure of our system if there were no reaction to such a blatant political move.
>
> Those who oppose these nominations are engaged in politics—but this is nonpartisan politics in the purest and finest sense.[10]

Senator George Murphy pointed out on the same day that there was no question of the President's power and right to make the appointments, but there was a question as to the propriety of his action. He associated the "unrest" in the nation with the Warren Court and the Johnson Administration, and implied that a new (presumably Republican) President would remedy the state of affairs:

> I can say, without equivocation, that this turbulence, this sense of unsureness, has been caused by some of the Court's recent decisions.
>
> I think it is most commendable that my colleague (Senator Griffin) has pointed out clearly that our opposition is not a matter of politics. More accurately it is a question of whether the President, under whose leadership this mental quandary of the people arose and under whose policies the people too often question, should appoint a new Supreme Court Justice and a new Chief Justice before the people of this great Nation have the opportunity at the polls in November to determine whether they want to change the course which we have been taking. . . . We do not question the power or the constitutional right of the President to make these appointments, but we do question the common sense and the judgment involved.[11]

As Senator Gore asked, if it is acknowledged that the President has the constitutional and legal right to make nominations and if the fitness, ability, and professional attainment of Fortas was not (at that

[10] *Congressional Records* July 11, 1968, p. S8506.
[11] *Ibid.*, p. S8514.

time) questioned, what then is the basis for opposition? "It adds up to the reluctance to agree to the confirmation of the nomination of Justice Fortas on the ground that it is a function that should be reserved for the next President."[12] This must be related either to partisan politics and the desire to reserve the appointment for a possible Republican President, or to a desire to alter the makeup of the Supreme Court and its position on several issues being discussed in the campaign, or a combination of both objectives.

Tactically, the manner of Warren's retirement was subject to criticism, but the issue was not central. There was in fact criticism of Warren on this very point from several supporters of Fortas. *The Progressive* termed it "less than adroit."[13] Alpheus T. Mason, in an article entitled "Pyrrhic Victory: The Defeat of Abe Fortas," observed that the opposition's politics was not unprovoked:

> On June 26, to the consternation of friends and enemies alike, Chief Justice Warren, in excellent health, announced his retirement, effective at such a time as a successor is qualified. Previously only two incumbents, John Jay and Charles Evans Hughes, seventy-nine, had voluntarily relinquished the position. All others either died in office, or continued until physically or mentally incapacitated.
>
> Critics deplored Warren's action as a nefarious plot concocted by the Chief Justice, President Johnson, and Justice Fortas to prevent replacement by the next President. It was argued that the Chief Justiceship should be kept open so that the incoming President, presumably Republican, could name Warren's successor. Against an enormous record to the contrary, the fantastic inference is that Johnson, the moment he withdrew his candidacy for re-election, lost the power to which President Taft gave top rating—the selection of Supreme Court Justices.[14]

Chief Justice Warren also came under severe attack from various leaders of the Republican Party. Spiro Agnew, then Governor of Maryland and Vice-Presidential candidate, charged that Warren did a terrible disservice to the Republican Party by not timing his resignation so that a new President could select his successor. Furthermore, Agnew said that Warren owed his appointment to the Republican

[12] *Ibid.*, p. S8515.
[13] "Covering the Court," *Progressive*, November, 1968, pp. 6–7.
[14] Mason, *op. cit.*

Party and, therefore, should have been loyal to his benefactors by withholding his resignation until a Republican could act upon it. *The Washington Post* in one of its frequent editorials attacking Fortas' critics in general, and Agnew in particular, accused Agnew of "lambasting the Chief Justice for not playing politics with his eminent judicial office. But the worst aspect of this Agnew comment is the implication that the Chief Justice of the United States should be guided by a sense of obligation as a Republican appointee."[15] It is interesting to note that some federal justices and judges have in the past been guided by a sense of obligation to the party instrumental in gaining them their judicial post. Justice Nathan Clifford, the last appointee of President Buchanan, remained tenaciously in his Supreme Court post, hoping to last long enough to be replaced by a Democratic President.[16] Clifford failed, but in 1969, Court of Appeals Judge John A. Danaher succeeded in restoring selection of his judicial seat to the party which had bestowed it upon him 15 years earlier. In 1953, John Danaher, former Republican senator from Connecticut, GOP fund raiser, and lobbyist, received President Dwight D. Eisenhower's first federal appellate court appointment, to the U.S. Court of Appeals for the District of Columbia. Danaher's nomination was publicized one day before President Eisenhower's announcement of Governor Earl Warren's nomination for Chief Justice of the United States. The sequel to Danaher's success in getting the coveted Court of Appeals post came in December of 1968 when he announced that although currently eligible he would retire after January 20, 1969, so that President-elect Nixon could fill the vacancy. Danaher stated candidly that he considered it "entirely fitting for me to return the vacancy" to the Republican Party.[17]

The "lame duck" issue provided a broader basis for counterattacks on the Republican opponents of Fortas. *The Washington Post*, on September 8, strongly criticized Senator Griffin and Spiro Agnew on the lame duck issue:

> The idea that President Johnson should have abstained from nominating a new Chief Justice in order to allow the next President to make the choice ought to be understood for what it is: a phony

[15] "Who is Being Insensitive?" *Washington Post*, September 30, 1968.

[16] Phillip Greeley Clifford, *Nathan Clifford, Democrat* (New York: G. Putnam & Sons, 1922), pp. 5, 331.

[17] John P. MacKenzie, "Danaher Returns GOP Favor," *Washington Post*, Sunday, December 8, 1948, pp. D1, D14.

gimmick, so alien to American tradition, so devastating to the operations of the Supreme Court, so open to retaliation that it can only be a smoke screen behind which politicians hide their animosity toward the President or their real reasons for opposing Mr. Fortas.

The idea promulgated by Governor Agnew that the current situation is all the fault of Chief Justice Warren is the same kind of gimmick. Since the summer is the only time a member of the Supreme Court can leave it without disrupting its activities, the full implication of the Governor's comment is that a justice is denied the right to retire in presidential election years regardless of his age or personal inclination.[18]

There was considerable historical support for the *Post*'s position. Presidents Washington, Adams, Jefferson, J. Q. Adams, Van Buren, Tyler, Fillmore, Buchanan, Hayes, Cleveland, Harrison, Taft, Wilson, Hoover, F. D. Roosevelt, and Eisenhower all had made election-year appointments. Five of the 96 men who sat on the bench were confirmed by the Senate although they were nominated by a President who had already been voted out of office. On only one occasion since the Civil War had the Senate refused to confirm a nomination made by a President during an election year, notably President Hayes' nomination of Stanley Matthews two months after the 1880 election. Of the 19 men rejected by the Senate, 12 were involved in the frequent struggles between the President and the Senate during the period from 1830 to 1870. Only one had met such a fate in the 20th century.

Senator Griffin and his fellow Republican opponents of Fortas also came under strong attack from several Southern senators who were actually opposed to the Fortas nomination. Senator Byrd, in a lengthy speech in opposition to Fortas, criticized those who argued that:

> because President Johnson asserted on March 31 that he would not be a candidate for re-election, he therefore is a lame duck President and should not submit nominations for the Federal Judiciary. I do not agree with such a view. To argue that he can't make appointments defies logic. The Senate's responsibility, as I see it, is to meet the issue head on, to deal squarely with the qualifications and the philosophy of the appointee. . . .[19]

[18] "The President, the Senate and the Court," *Washington Post*, September 8, 1968.

[19] *Congressional Record*, September 9, 1968, p. S10487.

Senator Smathers of Florida early in the debate put the "lame duck" question in another perspective. He stated:

> those Senators who whould deny the President the right and duty to appoint a successor to Chief Justice Warren should explain why they have unanimously approved at least 11 judicial nominations by the President since he announced his withdrawal from the Presidential race.[20]

Senator Smathers concluded by pointing out that President Eisenhower had nominated Justice William Brennan to the Supreme Court in October of 1956, one month prior to the Presidential election.

There was very little discussion in the Congress of Chief Justice Warren's thoughts on the "lame duck" issue or the controversy surrounding his retirement letter. Yet this information was readily available early in the debate from Warren's press conference of July 5. Commenting on the reasons he had chosen to use the language "at your pleasure," which was criticized severely by Senator Griffin and others, Warren had replied:

> For two or three reasons; there are 2 or 3 things involved in it. One of them is there always ought to be a Chief Justice of the United States because the Court is a continuous body and should have the leadership it is entitled to have.
>
> There is a lot of administrative work that happens with it, and if I selected a particular day, and if the vacancy was not filled it would be a vacuum. And our Court is in a different position than any other court in the land that I know anything about, in that if there is a vacancy you operate with eight men. There is no such thing as having a pro tem Justice on the Supreme Court. I felt that in retiring toward the end of the term that way, and leaving it to the convenience of the President, that it would provide for the continuity in office that is so important here and in the entire judiciary. There are a great many men retired from the judiciary who have done the same thing. They haven't put it to the President, but they have said when my successor is qualified, which is exactly the same thing . . . as my language to the President.[21]

Warren underscored his position in the news conference by saying he would not have any reservations about scheduling his retirement one month before a Presidential election "for the simple

[20] *Congressional Record*, July 1, 1968, p. S8047.
[21] U.S. Senate Committee of the Judiciary, *op. cit.*, p. 1383.

reason I think a Chief Justice should indicate his intention for retirement at the end of a term. . . ."[22]

Finally, the Chief Justice commented on the "lame duck" issue:

> QUESTION: Would you care to comment on President Johnson, as a lame duck President, naming your successor?
>
> ANSWER: I don't think the President is a lame duck President, as you termed it. The people of the United States enacted a Constitutional amendment saying that every President who served a second term cannot succeed himself. Do you consider that to be a lame duck President?[23]

THE WARREN COURT AND THE FORTAS CONTROVERSY

The debate soon took on the appearance of a full-scale partisan political battle. An examination of the *Congressional Record* makes it clear that decisions of the Warren Court and Justice Fortas' positions on controversial issues were very much a part of the controversy. In fact, the ongoing political campaign and the record of the Warren Court were closely related because criticism of several Warren Court decisions was an integral part of Republican campaign strategy. Presidential candidate Richard M. Nixon often attacked the Court's record and referred to the "barbed wire of legalism erected by the Supreme Court" to thwart law enforcement efforts. Furthermore, the Court was central to the debate over "law and order" in election campaigns at various levels of government and in most, if not all, parts of the country. Thus, it is difficult to separate the issue of the Court's record from the political campaign.

There is considerable evidence to suggest that dissatisfaction with the Warren Court was crucial to the desire to have a Republican President appoint the new Chief Justice. James Kilpatrick, a leading opponent of both the Warren Court majority and Justice Fortas, made the association quite clear when he expressed doubts about the ultimate defeat of Fortas:

> if the political argument depended solely upon a partisan charge of cronyism or upon the feeble proposition that an outgoing Presi-

[22] *Ibid.*, p. 1384.
[23] *Ibid.*

dent ought not to exercise his constitutional power of appointment, the argument would be worthless. . . . The Senate has every right to rebuke Warren for his devious attempt to assure the nomination of a successor he regards as suitably liberal. Warren started this whole business; he was the one who proposed to play politics with his high office, and he ought to be slapped down. . . . If challenges, based upon politics and propriety are not enough, Senators have every right—given this opportunity—to base their decision upon principles of constitutional construction. It is nonsense to contend, as some of Fortas' defenders are contending, that this is none of the Senate's business. This is precisely the Senate's business.[24]

Senator Strom Thurmond, one of the 19 Republican senators who signed the initial declaration of opposition to Fortas, indicated his keen interest in judicial philosophy in a Senate speech in July.

I signed the statement because it is my judgment that if President Johnson appoints a Chief Justice, he will not be the kind of judge who will stand for the Constitution and the principles of government on which this country was founded. . . . I believe that Chief Justice Warren colluded with the President of the United States to make that appointment now rather than waiting until a Republican was elected President, because they both want to continue the policies of Chief Justice Warren.[25]

Despite efforts to focus on other points, the *Congressional Record* is replete with articles and speeches attacking decisions of the Warren Court, particularly those related to "law and order," subversives, pornography, and the general charge of "judicial lawmaking" in a wide range of areas. Most of the comments by Southern senators exhibited candor similar to that of Senator Thurmond and are in direct contrast to the more indirect statements of their Northern colleagues on both sides of the issue.

Senator Hollings typified the Southern approach.

A vote for the confirmation of his [Fortas'] nomination as Chief Justice can only be taken as approving that brand [activism] of judicial philosophy.[26]

The Southern spokesmen charged repeatedly that Republican opponents of Fortas were "clouding the issue of judicial philoso-

[24] James Kilpatrick, *Washington Star*, September 15, 1968.
[25] *Congressional Record*, July 1, 1968, p. S8052.
[26] *Congressional Record*, July 18, 1968, p. S8855.

phy." They also criticized senators for not having fulfilled their Constitutional responsibility to conduct a searching ideological inquiry when Fortas was first nominated to the Court. That the dissatisfaction with the Court on the part of Republican opponents basically was not substantially dissimilar can be seen from the newspaper articles and editorials which these senators placed in the *Congressional Record.* For example, Senator Williams of Delaware inserted the following editorial from the *Wall Street Journal*:

> The Court, Mr. Warren and Mr. Johnson all have been playing politics for all it is worth. All three have been using every means at their disposal to make sure the judicial branch advances their social and economic views. Why should anyone be surprised that those who oppose the views in question also start playing politics, start using whatever means they can find to see that those views do not prevail?[27]

Debate over the judicial philosophy of a Chief Justice nominee may occur any time. However, when the nominee is a sitting justice the issue is most conducive to conflict. He has a public record on a broad range of issues, some of which may be extremely controversial. As pointed out previously, promotion of a sitting justice has been infrequent. Presidents Lincoln and Grant are said to have initiated a tradition, unbroken until 1910, of not elevating a justice. Mason suggests that Lincoln and Grant believed it would preclude undue rivalry within the Court. Furthermore, the tradition greatly reduces the potential for bitter struggle in the Senate.[28]

Several of Fortas' Senate supporters implied that the Senate had no business agreeing or disagreeing with the Justice's performance on the Court. The argument was that the Senate should examine the "professional competence" of the nominee and, presumably, the character of the nominee, but not his philosophy or convictions. Interestingly enough, Alexander Bickel, writing in the *New Republic*, cut the ground from under Fortas' Senate supporters by invoking the principle of consistency. Bickel argued that by this line of reasoning it was wrong for the Senate in 1930 to deny confirmation to Judge John J. Parker as Associate Justice simply because some of his decisions were ideologically unacceptable:

[27] "In re Mr. Justice Fortas," *The Wall Street Journal*, September 11, 1968, in *Congressional Record*, September 12, 1967, p. S10641.

[28] Mason, *op. cit.*, p. 20.

> This position is untenable. It reminds us of a time around the turn of the century when conservative opinion deified the Court as the neutral exponent of immutable constitutional principles, all of which happily protected property and the status quo, and called only for the professional skill of the lawyer to be properly declared and applied. Any inquiry that went beyond the establishment of a nominee's qualifications and into his beliefs was therefore not only unnecessary, but an insult to the man, impugning his competence and his integrity, and a vote against a nominee was rank Populist heresy and subversion of the Constitution. But when Wilson nominated Brandeis in 1916, the cat came out of the bag. All those same conservatives were horror-stricken, and opposed Brandeis despite his competence as a lawyer, because they found his convictions distasteful. Well neither Brandeis' opponents nor Justice Fortas' proponents can have it both ways. Judges make policy, and Brandeis' policy was different from that of Van Devanter and McReynolds and all those whom the conservatives of the day did not oppose; and Justice Fortas' policy is different from that of Senators Strom Thurmond and Sam Ervin, and nothing is more centrally relevant to his confirmation.[29]

The Southern senators accepted this viewpoint and pursued it publicly. In contrast, Northern senators on both sides of the nomination issue did not for the most part acknowledge, at least publicly, the relevance of judicial philosophy. However, its importance can be implied from their statements. For example, Senator Griffin said on August 22, 1968:

> When debating nominations for the Supreme Court, the Senate has never hesitated to look beyond mere qualifications to consider a nominee's philosophy, his writings, his views on issues, or other matters.[30]

Griffin pointed out that qualification or fitness was an issue in only four of the twenty-one instances in which the Senate had rejected Presidential nominations of Supreme Court Justices.

In contrast, the *Washington Post* on September 6, 1968, called for Senate confirmation of Fortas and severely criticized Senators Ervin and Thurmond for raising the issue of Fortas' philosophy.

[29] Bickel, *op. cit.*, p. 22.
[30] *Congressional Record*, August 22, 1968, p. E7557.

> If confirmation of a judicial nomination is made dependent upon the nominee's agreement with a majority of the Senate, that majority will obviously be able to exercise a controlling influence on the Court. It emphatically ought not to do so.[31]

The general argument was that judicial philosophy is not an appropriate issue for the Senate to consider and to do so would "compromise" the independence of the Supreme Court.

Senator McGee on September 22, 1968, inserted in the *Congressional Record* a statement which scorned Fortas' opponents for disguising their true reasons which were "partisanship and objections to civil rights." He then raised the issue of judicial philosophy by stating:

> Furthermore, contrary to charges that have been leveled against the nomination, I believe an impartial analysis of the opinions written by Justice Fortas will disclose that he has a well-developed sense of judicial restraint that clearly sets him apart from those members of the Court who have been constantly criticized as activist Justices in recent years. . . . If members of the Senate will pause to examine the voting record of Justice Fortas, they will find a Justice whose views are characterized by a keen awareness of the forces at work in society today. . . . I submit that both the qualifications and judicial philosophy of Justice Fortas amply merit his confirmation. . . .[32]

Senator Montoya took a similar approach early in the debate in a speech entitled "Justice Abe Fortas, A Man of Moderation" in which he discussed the voting record of Justice Fortas. His focus was on Fortas' positions on business and economic issues.[33] One of the most elaborate legally-oriented statements by a Fortas supporter was inserted in the *Congressional Record* on July 25, 1968, by Senator Gore. The presentation was a lengthy discussion of Fortas' position in a single case, *Katzenbach* v. *Morgan*, which upheld the constitutionality of section 4e of the Voting Rights Act of 1965 involving literacy and the Spanish language.[34] Senator Gore's discussion involved the relevance of judicial philosophy, although his defense was presented more broadly.

31 "The Senate and the Supreme Court," *Washington Post*, September 6, 1968.
32 *Congressional Record*, September 23, 1968, pp. S11204–5.
33 *Congressional Record*, July 25, 1968, pp. S8222–3.
34 *Congressional Record*, July 25, 1968, pp. S9380–1.

SEPARATION OF POWERS AND "CRONYISM"

Justice Fortas came under heavy attack for his widely reported role as a personal advisor to President Johnson. This phase of the controversy was closely related to the Justice's long-standing friendship with President Johnson, dating from the time Fortas represented the President in his legal battle for the 1948 Texas senatorial nomination. The debate over the issue of separation of powers and the Justice's services to the President bore little resemblance to a serious discussion of the constitutional issue. Rather it more frequently centered on the charge of "cronyism" and was intimately related to the preceding discussion of partisan politics. Senator Griffin, on July 11, 1968, associated the issues of cronyism and politics by stating:

> At a time when there is a desperate need to restore respect for law and order, as well as respect for the institutions which bear responsibility for maintaining law and order, the cause is not well served by nominations to the Highest Court which can be branded as cronyism—and legitimately so.[35]

Because one of the major issues of the 1968 campaign was "law and order," the implication to even a casual political observer was most obvious. The Senator concluded his speech with the insertion of a series of editorials, typified by one from *The Port Huron Times Herald*, carried on July 2, 1968, and entitled "Too Important for Cronyism." The tone of the editorial was set by a quotation from Senator Griffin which said, "The appointment announced smacks of 'cronyism' at its worst and everybody knows it."

Senator Hollings, although opposed to Fortas, rejected the "cronyism" argument as without merit, with the candor typifying much of the debate by Southern senators.

> After 31 years in Government, President Johnson . . . must have made some cronies. Obviously many of them were men of talent, and who would penalize a man of talent simply because he was a friend. Certainly not a member of the U.S. Senate from whence the springwell of cronyism flows. There are members sitting in this body now who arrived here via the appointment route. And I suspect that they were appointed not by a political enemy, but by a crony. And how many of us have appointed friends and former

[35] *Congressional Record*, July 11, 1968, p. S8506.

law partners to judgeships? The number, I am sure, would run into the hundreds.[36]

Senator Hollings then pointed out that of 321 judges appointed during the Eisenhower Administration, 13 were Democrats. He concluded:

No one faults these appointments by President Eisenhower as cronyism. No. Mr. President, cronyism is not the issue.[37]

There is little evidence to the contrary in the public record. However, from a partisan political viewpoint the issue of cronyism presumably had some public appeal. With the President's standing with the public at a low level, with past controversies over several of his political associates—e.g., Walter Jenkins—still in mind, and his long-standing and often-commented-upon reputation of political manipulation, the charge of cronyism was not difficult to project as relevant to the controversy. In fact, the insertions in the *Congressional Record* suggest the issue was utilized by a sizable portion of the nation's editorial writers, particularly editors of smaller circulation newspapers.

Crucial to the Congressional discussion of cronyism and separation of powers was Fortas' widely reported role as a personal advisor to President Johnson. Senator Griffin made the point clear on July 11, 1968, when he initiated his discussion of separation of powers with a direct reference to cronyism. Many of the press reports of Fortas' advisory relationship with the President were inserted in the *Congressional Record* by Senator Griffin and other opponents of the Justice. Their general tone hardly supported Harry Truman's observation that "Whenever you put a man on the Supreme Court, he ceases to be your friend."[38] Senator Griffin also charged Fortas with working on behalf of various individuals to secure particular appointments—Bill Moyers for Under Secretary of State, David G. Bress for a federal judgeship, to name but two—and of advising the President on steel-price increases, transportation strikes, Vietnam and foreign policy, the Warren Commission, the Johnson family-trust agreement, and the Walter Jenkins affair. Furthermore, the Senator inserted an item from the July 5, 1968, issue

[36] *Congressional Record*, September 25, 1968, p. S11378.
[37] *Ibid.*
[38] *Congressional Record*, July 11, 1970, p. S8506.

of *Time* magazine which reported that Fortas wrote the President's message ordering federal troops into Detroit during the 1967 riot. *Time* quoted no less an authority than the President, who reportedly said in response to criticism of the statement and with reference to Fortas, "Why, I had the best Constitutional lawyer in the United States right here, and he wrote that."[39]

Justice Fortas' extrajudicial activity was attacked on several grounds, including desirability from a Constitutional viewpoint. However, it was not lacking in historic antecedents. Alpheus T. Mason offered the observation that

> . . . during the Federalist era, politicians and statesmen bivouacked in and out of the Chief Justiceship on their march from one position to another. For six months John Jay held simultaneously the offices of Chief Justice and Secretary of State. Jay ran for the governorship of New York while still on the bench. He served for a year as Chief Justice and Ambassador to England. For eighteen months Oliver Ellsworth was Minister to France while still retaining the Chief Justiceship. Without relinquishing his judicial post, Associate Justice Cushing ran for governor of Massachusetts. Justice Bushrod Washington was openly active in the presidential campaign of 1800. John Marshall continued as Secretary of State for a month after his appointment as Chief Justice.[40]

It was difficult to make a case against extrajudicial activities on the basis of lack of precedent. Mason made the point that Roger Brooke Taney served as President Jackson's one-man brain trust, advising the President on various policy matters and writing speeches including his farewell address. More recently, Louis Brandeis served as a consultant to President Wilson and although, as Mason points out, "both were sensitive to judicial proprieties, neither was deterred from communications calculated to promote the public good."

Chief Justice Taft was deeply involved with—among others—Presidents Harding and Coolidge and sought to influence not only their policies but also the course of action for the Republican party. Nor did Charles Evans Hughes hesitate to communicate with the legislative branch his strong opposition to President Franklin D. Roosevelt and the New Deal. Nor was there much concern expressed by Justice Frankfurter when he came under attack for advising Franklin Roosevelt. Furthermore, although Justice Stone expressed

[39] *Congressional Record*, July 11, 1968, p. 58506.
[40] Mason, *op. cit.*, pp. 22–23.

his anger at Roosevelt's attempt to use him in an advisory capacity, Mason points out correctly that he had not been so "fastidious" in his relationship with President Hoover.[41] The practice continued during the Truman Administration as the President was reported to have often relied on the counsel of Chief Justice Vinson. Finally, Warren's tenure was not devoid of extrajudicial activity as he traveled to several parts of the world in the capacity of good-will ambassador and served as the head of the Commission to investigate the assassination of President John F. Kennedy. On the matter of historic practice, Senator Wayne Morse stated:

> The record speaks clearly and proudly of almost 200 years of our history. It speaks of Presidents, Republicans, and Democrats alike, who have sought and received advice and counsel from members of the Supreme Court in whom they trusted and confided. . . . Is there a single member of this body—of the separate legislative branch—who would refuse to give advice and counsel to the President? Is there a single member of this body who has not been in the White House to consult on some matter?[42]

The Senator then directed his attention to Senator Griffin—and implicitly the Senate in general—with the assertion that "Senator Griffin can counsel the President and recommend actions to him on a riot situation in Detroit, but a Supreme Court Justice is not even permitted to read a President's statement about the riots, according to this unfortunate rationale."[43]

Senator Griffin chose to use as historical authority the response of the Supreme Court to President George Washington's request for advice which was made through his Secretary of State, Thomas Jefferson. The Court said:

> We have considered the previous question stated . . . regarding the lines of separation, drawn by the Constitution between the three departments of government. These being in certain respects checks upon each other, and our being Judges of a court in the last resort, are considerations which afford strong arguments against the propriety of our extra-judicially deciding the questions alluded to, especially as the power given by the Constitution to the President, of calling on the heads of departments for opinions, seems to

[41] *Ibid.*, pp. 24–27.
[42] *Congressional Record*, July 18, 1968, *p*. 58910.
[43] *Ibid.*

have been purposely as well as expressly united in the Executive departments.[44]

This historical reference to the formal distinction between branches was hardly of the same nature as the previously discussed informal activities of individual justices. Alpheus Mason believed that concern over the question of separation of powers was directly related to the concern on the part of some members of Congress that the institution was losing power to both the President and the judiciary. This was evidenced in the establishment in 1967 of a subcommittee on Separation of Powers of the Senate Committee on the Judiciary to study the question and to "search for legislative proposals, where necessary, to restore the three branches to their proper Constitutional roles and preclude encroachments by one branch upon the process and functions of another." There is little doubt that Senator Ervin believed the Court's tendency to "make law" had contributed to this alteration of the federal system. Mason suggested that the Subcommittee study was directly related to Ervin's drive against Fortas.[45] If his interpretation is accurate, and the comments found in the *Congressional Record* support him, this source of opposition to Fortas also was based, at least partially, on dissatisfaction with the Warren Court. Once again, as with each of the issues raised in opposition to the nominee, Southern opponents of Fortas emphasized the fundamental basis for the dispute, namely, the Warren Court's record of judicial activism and Fortas' role in the writing of that record.

Pornography and "Peep Shows"

Several senators, such as Strom Thurmond and Jack Miller, attacked Justice Fortas' alleged "soft line" on pornography. Of particular concern to this group was the justice's vote to reverse the conviction of one Harry Schackman and five associates by a jury in Los Angeles for violating California's state law against the exhibition of obscene motion pictures. The Superior Court of California upheld Schackman's conviction. However, the United States Supreme Court, on June 12, 1967, in a per curiam decision, reversed *Schackman* v. *California*. A similar case, *Jacobs* v. *New York*, was dismissed on the

[44] *Congressional Record*, July 11, 1968, p. S8507.
[45] Mason, *op. cit.*, p. 23.

same day. Together the cases formed the basis for attacks on Justice Fortas' attitude on pornography.

Mr. James J. Clancy presented the issue as spokesman for The Citizens for Decent Literature. Clancy's statement was inserted in the *Congressional Record* by Congressman John R. Rarick of Louisiana and was quoted by numerous Fortas opponents. In testimony before the Committee, Clancy related the pornography rulings to court decisions in the criminal law field and to the general charge of "judicial activism."

> The common issue in all of these recent court storm centers is whether the judgments of the Court are grounded upon constitutional principle or upon the personal judgments of the individual members.[46]

This position was taken by Senator Jack Miller of Iowa, who associated pornography decisions with the Warren Court's record in several subject matter areas including crime and internal security. Senator Miller served on the national advisory board of Citizens for Decent Literature and on July 22, 1968, used the Committee's testimony to express his opposition to Fortas. The Senator described Fortas' judgment as encouraging, ". . . the permissiveness and criminal activity which are plaguing our society."[47]

The issue received considerable nationwide attention when Senator Strom Thurmond arranged for members of the Senate to view the film "0-7" which was involved with the Schackman Case. The *New Republic* later termed the Thurmond showing a "striptease peepshow film for other leering senators . . ." and labeled it ". . . one of the most obscene spectacles we have seen in Washington, worthy of Jonathan Swift's Yahoos."[48] In contrast, Senator Miller described the film as "hard core pornography" and urged other members of Congress and the press to ". . . avail themselves of this opportunity so that they will understand how serious this matter is."[49] The attacks on Fortas' record on pornography were further spiced by attacks by Congressmen Rarick and Ashbrook. Rarick stated:

> Mr. Speaker, Abe Fortas has earned his role as Mr. Obscenity based upon his extremist notions that the parents and society in

[46] *Congressional Record*, July 22, 1968, p. E6759.
[47] *Congressional Record*, July 26, 1968, p. S9440.
[48] "Shadow on the Court," *New Republic*, May 17, 1969.
[49] *Congressional Record*, July 26, 1968, p. S9440.

> general should have no power or right to establish a pattern of morals or dignity as to what constitutes decent literature.[50]

Congressman John Ashbrook, on September 5, 1968, chortled in reference to a theater ad in the *Washington Post*:

> Good ole Abe—just exactly the kind of man the stripteasers have been looking for. And now while they're changing the reels on to the next feature—oh well![51]

Supporters of Fortas countered the attack with a factual discussion of the justice's record on pornography cases. Their position was supported by an article written by Joseph O'Meara, dean emeritus of the Notre Dame Law School, and a frequent critic of Warren Court decisions. Dean O'Meara charged that the Fortas critics were unfair because they based their opposition on two cases which were decided without written opinion. He also concluded that the attack was misleading because it overlooked Fortas' total record in the field, which was described by Dean O'Meara as indicating a "commendable, judicious temperament wholly undeserving of the kind of attack which has been launched against him in the Senate." O'Meara termed "dangerous" the opposition's use of two per curiam decisions as a basis for the attack. The article, inserted in the *Congressional Record* by numerous supporters of Fortas, was endorsed by deans of the Boston College Law School, University of Arizona School of Law, Yale Law School, and Vanderbilt University School of Law.[52]

American University and The Seminar Fund

The charge of conflict of interest also was made by opponents of Justice Fortas. This controversy stemmed from his acceptance of a $15,000 fee for giving nine lectures to students at American University Law School, one of which ultimately was not given by Fortas but rather by Juvenile Court Judge Ketcham. The fee was paid from a $30,000 fund financed by five wealthy individuals who with their corporate interests had been clients of Fortas' law firm before the justice went to the Court. Dean Tenners of the Washington College of Law, American University, in testimony before the Senate Committee on the Judiciary testified that in his efforts to raise the fund, he

[50] *Congressional Record*, July 22, 1968, p. E6759.

[51] *Congressional Record*, September 5, 1968, p. E7706.

[52] "An Unfair Issue: Justice Fortas and Obscenity Cases," by Joseph O'Meara, *Washington Post*, September 11, 1968.

had "had the complete and enthusiastic cooperation of Paul A. Porter," a former law firm associate of Justice Fortas. The Dean defended American University's legal seminar program and expressed his satisfaction with Fortas' participation in it. Under extensive questioning, particularly by Senators Thurmond and McClellan, Dean Tenners argued that Fortas was "probably the finest man you could find for this position. . . ."[53]

The conflict of interest charge was argued in Congress in a manner suggesting it was not of primary concern to either the opponents or supporters of Fortas. The latter acknowledged "indiscretion" but spent little time on the issue. The former, particularly those critical of the Justice's pornography decision, attempted to use the charge as an illustration of Fortas' alleged lack of sound judgment and as a basis for several attacks on the Warren Court and the behavior of several of its justices. The relatively late date of emergence of the conflict of interest charge may well have been a factor in the minor role it played. The absence of a strong code of ethics for the Senate with regard to outside income may well have inhibited fuller debate. In any event there is little evidence to suggest that the issue was central to the case against Fortas in 1968. It did contribute to the filibuster efforts by providing an additional topic, and it provided a reason for opposition that had potential appeal to voters, without the hazards of an openly partisan attack. It did however set the tone for future examinations of ethical questions involving judicial officials. The first to experience this was Fortas himself.

The Cloture Vote

After several months of prolonged debate, the Senate, on October 1, 1968, defeated 45–43 a motion to stop debate on the motion to take up the nomination of Abe Fortas to be Chief Justice of the United States. On October 3, Senator Mike Mansfield inserted in the *Congressional Record* a statement to the press on Justice Fortas' request to President Johnson that his nomination be withdrawn.

Any analysis of cloture is subject to severe hazards because of the difficulty of interpreting the true meaning of a senator's vote. Senator Kuchel made this clear by pointing out on the day of the vote that it was not on the merits of the Fortas nomination but on a procedural motion to take up the nomination. In fact, there is some evidence to

[53] "Hearings," *op. cit.*, p. 1304.

suggest that the vote was not an actual count of support or opposition to Justice Fortas. For example, Senator John Sherman Cooper pointed out that he supported cloture but would oppose Fortas if the matter came to a vote. It is quite possible that other senators harbored similar views. However, as Senator Mansfield pointed out:

> For the first time the Senate—or more accurately, a minority of Senators—would frustrate the Senate's constitutional obligation on questions of nominations. For the first time, the device of a filibuster would be used to bring down a Presidential nominee.
>
> But the simple fact is a filibuster has never occurred before on a nomination submitted by the President. . . . In the past the Senate has discussed, debated, at times agonized, but always it has voted on the merits. No Senator or group of Senators has ever usurped that constitutional prerogative.[54]

The question whether or not to take a vote on the nomination had become an issue in and of itself. For example, a nationwide committee of lawyers had been formed to push for a vote without comment on the merits of the nomination. The Committee was strongly critical of the filibuster and attacked Senator Griffin and supporters for "making a mockery of the constitutional process."[55]

An analysis of the vote does suggest several things. First, those supporting cloture were, with few exceptions, all Northern Democrats or Republicans from large industrial states with moderate to liberal voting records, as defined by the *New Republic* and other similar indexes. For example, of the ten Republican senators supporting cloture all but two, Kuchel and Dominick, received relatively high ratings in the *New Republic* scorecard on the 90th Congress.[56] Taking into consideration absences, the eight other senators supported the *New Republic* position on a minimum of 70% of the votes, with Senators Case and Hatfield supporting that position on each of the 12 votes.[57] Senator Kuchel supported the *New Republic* position on 4 of 10 votes (2 absences) and Senator Dominick, 3 of 10 votes. In spite of this rather low rating, Senator Kuchel's reputation was that of a moderate Republican, a fact which contributed to his defeat in

[54] *Congressional Record*, October 1, 1968, p. S11684 and S11686.

[55] *Congressional Record*, September 13, 1968, p. S10732.

[56] "The C+ Congress . . . key votes in the 90th," *New Republic*, November 2, 1968, pp. 21–28.

[57] Senator Goodell did not take office until late in the session and voted on only one issue.

the 1968 California senatorial primary. It is not clear why Senator Dominick supported cloture, but one possible source of influence on the senator may have been the position of the *Denver Post*, which on September 8, 1968, expressed strong support for Fortas and urged the Senate to stay in session as long as necessary to win confirmation.[58] Finally, an analysis of 9 votes taken in the 90th Congress (detailed in Chapter 7) which either overturned Supreme Court decisions or attempted to alter the Court's jurisdiction reveals a pro-Court position on the majority of the roll calls by each of the Republican senators supporting cloture.

Of the three Northern Democratic senators opposing cloture—Dodd, Lausche, and Cannon—at least two had been identified as conservatives within the Northern wing of the Democratic party. For example, of the 12 votes recorded by the *New Republic*, Senators Lausche and Cannon voted positively four times, with Senator Cannon absent on 2 votes.[59] Senator Lausche took an anti-Court or anti-Court-decision position on 5 roll calls, and Senator Cannon on 7 of the 9 votes examined from the 90th Congress.

Senator Dodd's record is closer to the party's majority position on both indexes. He voted with the *New Republic* position on 6 of 9 votes and took an anti-Court position on just 3 of the 9 votes. An explanation of Senator Dodd's voting behavior is not clear from an examination of the *Congressional Record*. However, on the basis of his past critical statements about Supreme Court decisions related to Communists and other "subversives," it does not seem unreasonable to suggest this dissatisfaction with the Court's record may have been a factor in his opposition to Fortas.

There were two Southern Democrats supporting cloture. Senator Yarborough had voted positively on the *New Republic* scale of 7 of 10 roll calls, and Senator Randolph had done so on 7 of 12 roll calls. Senators Randolph and Yarborough each supported the Court on 5 of 9 votes assessed for the 90th Congress.

The cloture vote, which required 59 votes to gain approval, clearly indicated the division between North and South in the Democratic party. Of the 36 Northern Democratic senators voting on the issue, 33 or approximately 90% voted for cloture. In contrast, 17 or 89% of the 19 senators from 11 southern states voted against the motion. Conversely, 10 Republican senators, or 26% of the 34

[58] "Fortas is Worth a Filibuster," *Denver Post*, September 8, 1968.
[59] "The C+ . . . key votes in the 90th," *op. cit.*

who voted on the issue, supported cloture. The successful voting alliance was composed of Southern Democrats and Republicans. Those Republicans who supported cloture were primarily representative of the moderate to liberal wing of the party, and the three northern Democrats opposing cloture were clearly in the more conservative wing of the party. Whatever labels one applies, the latter groups differed substantially from the great majority of their party colleagues in the Senate.

The Implications

The issues associated with the Fortas nomination and the diverse and sometimes complicated motives of the individual senators make it most difficult to generalize. However, as the preceding summary of the first Fortas controversy indicated, there is little doubt that the Fortas nomination presented the Senate with an opportunity to examine not just the nominee but also the Supreme Court and its record under Chief Justice Earl Warren. As on other occasions in the past, the potential for conflict between the two branches of the federal government was revealed clearly as the Senate sought to carry out its constitutional responsibility to "advise and consent" on Presidential nominations. In the process of doing so, the role and responsibilities of the institutions, never clearly defined, was a subject of much controversy. There is little, if any, doubt that the activism of the Warren Court was a factor in the defeat of Abe Fortas. The charge that the Court was "making laws" and thereby usurping legislative responsibilities was a matter of increasing concern to many members of the Congress who have witnessed its relative position in the federal system decline in importance, particularly with regard to the Executive. The political climate of 1968 provided ample opportunity for attacks on many of the controversial Court decisions of the preceding decade.

The Fortas nomination was viewed as a golden opportunity to "make political hay" by attacking the Supreme Court and its actions on the problems of the day. Repeatedly, the Court came under attack for "freeing murderers and hardened criminals" and "handcuffing law enforcement," permitting "peddlers of smut" to run loose in the community weakening "moral fiber," taking "God" out of the schools, and destroying local government with its reapportionment decisions as Congressional opponents attacked key decisions of the Warren Court. There is no question that the Court's efforts to expand constitutional protections for the unpopular and the politically weak segments of the population had greatly increased dissatisfaction with the Court. Professor Theodore Mitau accurately summed up its contributions in the introduction to his excellent book, *Decade of Decision: The Supreme Court and the Constitutional Revolution, 1954–1964*:

> During the past decade the Supreme Court of the United States rendered a number of critically important decisions which vastly expanded constitutional protections for the politically weak, the socially disliked and the criminally suspect. More than ever before, the Court forced majorities to extend consideration and respect to the rights of unpopular minorities and to their consensus—disrupting causes and conduct.[60]

Ironically, the very developments which earned the Warren Court the praise of its "attentive public" in academic halls and the meetings of urban lawyers' associations also hardened its political opposition. As a justice of the Warren Court who quite often supported the majority position, Fortas felt the full weight of the attack on the Court. This point was central to his defeat in 1968.

The second major factor in the rejection of the Fortas nomination was directly partisan rather than ideological. The campaign for the Presidency produced major frontal attacks on the Supreme Court and its record. The Republican Presidential and Vice-Presidential candidates repeatedly attacked the Court and called for a new type of court that would exercise "judicial restraint" and follow "precedent" in making decisions. Presidential candidate Richard M. Nixon pledged himself to appoint "strict constructionists" and "conservative jurists" who would not act as legislators. Thus, several ideological critics of the Court in the Senate (notably Southern Democrats) found in Richard M. Nixon a possible remedy for the situation. The Presidential candidate and his fellow Republicans in the Senate left little doubt that a nominee of a judicial persuasion different than Fortas would be forthcoming if the Republicans were successful in November. With public opinion polls and political observers pointing out the public's dissatisfaction with

[60] G. Theodore Mitau, *Decade of Decision: The Supreme Court and the Constitutional Revolution, 1954–1964* (New York: Charles Scribner's Sons, 1967), p. 3.

the Warren Court's decisions, such a position did have political appeal.

The Court's defenders, for the most part Northern Democrats in the Senate, supported the nominee and the Court while Court critics, conservatives for the most part, attacked Fortas. There is no doubt that the fight over the Fortas nomination was both partisan and ideological.

An additional point that is most clear from the analysis of the 1968 Fortas controversy is that when the Court is under severe attack for its decisions, as in the Parker fight of 1930, the nomination process is a ready-made battleground. In 1968 any nominee might have provoked substantial controversy. An increasing number of Senators had been openly attacking the Court since the early 1950s and, as analyses of the subsequent roll calls indicate, the Congress had become increasingly willing to overturn Court decisions and to vote affirmatively on drastic measures aimed at curbing the Court. In this climate, the nomination process is a natural and potentially very effective vehicle for attacking the Court. Historically, the relations between Congress and the Court has varied from intermittent guerrilla warfare to open conflict. When the state of affairs approximates the latter, as was the case in 1968, the nomination process provides a ready battleground for ideological and partisan conflict.

THE BITTER SEQUELS TO 1968

In May 1969, the second Fortas controversy began with the publication by *Life* magazine of a story charging the Associate Justice with accepting a $20,000 fee from the foundation of (then indicted, later convicted) financier Louis Wolfson in January, 1966, a few months after Fortas had been appointed to the Supreme Court. Congressman H. R. Gross of Iowa called for Fortas' impeachment. Leading opponents of Fortas in the Senate such as Robert Griffin of Michigan and John J. Williams of Delaware were severely critical; Senator Jack Miller of Iowa called for Fortas' resignation.[61] Nor was the criticism limited to old opponents. Fortas' strongest editorial support in the controversy of 1968 had come from the *Washington Post*. On May 6, 1969, the *Post* suggested that Justice Fortas "re-

[61] *Washington Post*, Monday, May 5, 1969, pp. A1 & A4; and Tuesday, May 6, 1969, pp. A1 & A6.

move" the "shadow" of possible inpropriety by full disclosure of his dealings with Wolfson. It concluded that,

> If Justice Fortas, however, cannot remove that shadow more persuasively, he must take the drastic and painful step of protecting the Court from his indiscretions. The Court stands today, as it frequently has in the past, in the middle of a storm—this one centering on the issue of "law and order." It will need all the respect and all the support it can get if the forthright positions it itself has staked out in the last 15 years on issues of due process are not to be undermined. As a participant in the formulation of some of those positions and as a defender of the Court in the days before he sat upon it, Justice Fortas must recognize the need that its integrity stand unblemished. . . .[62]

A few days later Justice Fortas resigned from the Supreme Court. Interviewed by Benjamin C. Bradlee, Fortas said "If I stayed on the Court, there would be this constitutional confrontation that would go on for months. Hell, I feel there wasn't any choice for a man of conscience."[63]

Fortas' resignation highlighted ethical requirements for Supreme Court service, but the forces most influential in the nominating process appeared to many observers to be most attuned to the ideological and sectional issues of subsequent political campaigns. Many members of the Senate remembered vividly the dramatic occasion during the Senate Judiciary Committee hearings on the Fortas' nomination for Chief Justice of the United States when Senator Strom Thurmond of South Carolina shouted: "Mallory! Mallory! I want that name to ring in your ears."

Thus when President Nixon nominated Court of Appeals Judge Clement Haynsworth of South Carolina, the President displayed far greater interest in the ideological and electoral calculus than in the ethical implications of the nomination. And for many weeks it appeared that this insensitivity to ethics would have little effect on the outcome of the Senate nomination vote despite the moving testimony of several Haynsworth opponents. The necessity to raise the "deplorably low standard of judicial ethics" was, indeed, presented as the reason for the organization of one of the testifying groups,

[62] *Washington Post*, Tuesday, May 6, 1969, p. A18.

[63] *Washington Post*, Friday, May 16, 1969, p. A1. For a full account of the second Fortas controversy see the preliminary portion of Thomas Halper, "Supreme Court Responses to Congressional Threats: Strategy and Tactics," *19 Drake Law Review* (May, 1970), especially pp. 293–342.

"The Committee for a Fair, Honest, and Impartial Judiciary."[64] However, ideological opposition to a potential backward shift on civil rights was important as well. A notable example was the testimony of Professor Gary Orfield of Princeton who said on September, 26, 1969, that

> One of the remarkable things about this year, to a student of school desegregation, is the ease with which actions unthinkable a year ago have become commonplace. Each week seems to bring a further retreat by the executive branch in civil rights enforcement. The Justice Department, so long in the forefront of the battle to enforce Constitutional guarantees, has succeeded in postponing desegregation in Mississippi schools. The House has passed, with Administration support, an amendment that would destroy what remains of HEW'S school desegregation program. Now the newspapers report that few Senators are worried about putting on the Supreme Court a backward-looking judge from a Circuit Court with a very poor record in protecting civil rights.[65]

The defeat of Haynsworth and the subsequent nomination and defeat of Harrold Carswell were in turn followed by the anticlimactic nomination and confirmation of Circuit Judge Harry Blackmun. Throughout these nomination controversies basic questions involving ethical standards for the federal judiciary were, as in the two Fortas conflicts, seemingly inexorably interwoven. Again and again in heated political discourse, the question was raised whether the invocation of ethical objections to Haynsworth or qualitative objections against Carswell was ostensible rather than real? Did the opponents of these Nixon nominees basically object to them on ideological and political grounds? There is little doubt that the impact of the Fortas' controversies upon the next two nominations was substantial. Former Congressional Quarterly researcher Spencer Rich provided support for this view near the climax of the Haynsworth controversy. Rich argued, on November 16, 1969, that,

> It has long been Senate practice to "give the President his man" on major appointments—even where Senators did not agree with the man's philosophy—provided he is honest and qualified

[64] See the Testimony of Randolph Phillips before the Senate Judiciary Committee in *Hearings on the Nomination of Clement F. Haynsworth, Jr.*, September 26, 1969, p. 541.

[65] Gary Orfield in Testimony before the Senate Judiciary Committee, *op. cit.*, p. 554.

> for office. But much of the restraining influence of that tradition was lost when southerners ferociously attacked Fortas for his pro-civil rights stands and rulings in favor of the rights of criminal defendants. . . .[66]

Among Haynsworth's strongest Senate supporters were men who led the attacks in 1968 upon Abe Fortas—Strom Thurmond, James Eastland, John McClellan, and Sam Ervin. Rich also argued that the Fortas' ethical issues had made a profounder impact than many political and legal leaders suspected:

> To those familiar with the legal profession and the conduct of judges, Fortas' extrajudicial activities may well have been unremarkable. But these revelations came as a profound shock to wide segments of the public.

Rich also commented, prophetically as the events of the immediate future proved, that,

> Whatever the merits of all the arguments against Haynsworth, it seems clear in another time he would have been confirmed and with relatively little controversy.[67]

Several Fortas' opponents of 1968 voted against Haynsworth in 1969, including Senator Griffin of Michigan and Senator Miller of Iowa. Critics of Haynsworth were accused (as were subsequent critics of Carswell's qualifications) of utilizing one issue, here judicial ethics, to hide their actual ideological and partisan reasons for opposing him. Content analysis of legislative debates and the conduct of Congressmen in committee hearings can, as utilized by Harry Stumpf, provide insight concerning one mode of legislative behavior. Conversely, the question can be raised whether rhetorical attacks upon the Court, its decisions, or nominees or its members are actually reflected in the voting behavior of individual House and Senate members. By shifting emphasis from the tantalizing but exceedingly difficult task of speculating about motivation to the systematic measurement of actual voting behavior, consistent patterns of opposition or support by members of Congress can be identified. This analysis is the purpose of the subsequent chapter.

The aftermath of the Fortas controversies provides tangential support for greater emphasis upon measuring action rather than

[66] *Washington Post*, Sunday, November 16, 1969, p. B3.
[67] *Ibid.*

counting words. Despite the increased attention focused upon considerations of judicial propriety, neither the Congress nor the self-policing efforts of the Judicial Conference of the United States have succeeded in establishing truly strong standards of judicial ethics. Indeed, the stern requirements adopted by the Conference under Chief Justice Earl Warren in June, 1968, have been softened. Warren had pushed adoption of a resolution requiring the filing of confidential income and financial holding reports with the Conference. Outside work for pay required special permission from the judicial governing body of each federal circuit. Since 1968, these relatively strong standards have been relaxed by succeeding Judicial Conferences while Congress itself has failed to act on legislation proposed by Senator Tydings to fulfill the same purposes.

Ironically, many of the same kinds of ethical questions that have been raised in connection with Associate Justice William O. Douglas' role as president of the Albert Parvin Foundation are basic to the day-to-day conduct of judicial business in the federal judicial circuits. John R. MacKenzie's detailed analysis of the manner in which the monumental *Southern Louisiana Gas Rate Case* was handled by two (of three) circuit judges holding substantial personal or trusteeship portfolios in oil and gas (including some corporations which were parties to the suit) indicated the serious and fundamental nature of the problem.[68] Many Congressional opponents of Justice Douglas would, needless to say, enthusiastically attack him on ethical grounds, but, to date, have indicated little interest in the pervasive problem of raising *all* federal judicial standards. Thus, they tend to ignore the necessity for reform of conditions in some of the circuits such as the status of Federal Power Commission cases aptly described by MacKenzie:

> . . . Federal Power Commission rulings are reviewable in any one of several circuit courts, depending on which petitioner gets to which court first. Lawyers admit that it is unseemly but they routinely race to file their petitions with the circuit of their choice. Consumer groups favor the District of Columbia circuit, where the judges tend to favor the federal regulators against attacks by industry. But the producers love their home circuits, the Fifth in the Southeast and the 10th in the Southwest, where judges listen more attentively to the industries of their locales. [In the *Southern*

[68] John P. MacKenzie, "The Public is Starting to Judge Judges," *Washington Post*, Sunday, October 26, 1969, pp. B1 & B3.

> *Louisiana Gas Rate Case*] Producers won the race last spring because the Fifth circuit clock lacked a sweep second hand, requiring the clerk to assign a time just ahead of filings in Washington and Denver. [This byplay involved litigation in which $80 million dollars in yearly rate reductions, huge amounts of refunds, and the future of gas supplies for the Northeast and Midwest were at stake.][69]

Prior to this, Dean Acheson had presented a comprehensive judicial-ethics reform proposal in testimony before the Subcommittee on the Separation of Powers of the Senate Judiciary Committee. The Acheson plan (a) flatly forbids supplementing judicial salaries by outside earnings and limited lectures to "legal" subjects, (b) prohibited all nonjudicial work or special assignments (such as Presidential Commissions), (c) opposed political appointments of ex-judges unless a period of years elapsed since resignation from a judicial post, (d) opposed nomination of associate justices to the Chief Justiceship, and (e) prohibited private judicial advice to political office holders. Acheson also urged Congress to enact rules of judicial conduct into law and to increase the powers of the Judicial Conference to investigate and suspend federal judges and in serious situations recommend resignation.[70] These and similar recommendations have not been acted upon by either Congress or the Judicial Conference.

[69] *Ibid.*, p. B3.

[70] Dean Acheson, Testimony before the Subcommittee on the Separation of Powers, July 16, 1969, reproduced in *American Bar Association Journal* (October, 1969), pp. 919–921.

7

The Congress and the Court: Tradition v. Roll Call Analysis

The defeat of the Court-packing plan of President Franklin D. Roosevelt in the 1930s has had greater influence upon modern academic evaluations of the nature of Congressional attitudes toward the Court than any other single event. Indeed, many historians and political scientists accept with little question the assumption that the Court as an institution was revered by the American public as well as by a majority of members of Congress. Concerning the controversy of 1937, a variety of explanations have been provided for Roosevelt's defeat, including criticism of his tactics and the indirect manner in which he initially raised the issue. However, virtually every assessment of the Court-packing fight emphasized the reverence theme.

Were the words of praise showered upon the Court by Roosevelt's Congressional opponents during the Court-packing fight accurate indications of their commitment to the Court as an institution? Or were these arguments part and parcel of an emerging division, the stakes of which were primarily economic and political rather than constitutional? Were the florid rhetorical references of men like Senator Edward Burke of Nebraska reserved for a Supreme Court dedicated to the preservation of unregulated business or to a judicial institution which, within a few years, shifted its emphasis to the protection of numerous nonproperty rights? The language of Burke in 1937 was expansive—"Only a Supreme Court, independent and unawed, stands guard to protect the rights and liberties of the people."[1]

President Roosevelt claimed that while he lost the Supreme Court battle in 1937 he won the war. The historical evidence bears him out. Two and one half years after the defeat of his Court plan, Roosevelt appointed five new members of the Supreme Court, Hugo Black, Stanley Reed, Felix Frankfurter, William O. Douglas, and Frank Murphy. The new Roosevelt Court, "has not," in the words of a leading historian of the New Deal era, "invalidated a single piece of congressional legislation regulating business" since 1937. The same analyst, Professor William E. Leuchtenburg, concluded that, "Whereas the beneficiaries of the Court before 1937 had been businessmen and other propertied interests, after 1937 they became the less advantaged groups in America."[2] Allies of the business community among news-media influentials tended to agree with the appraisal made by Frank Gannett in February, 1938: "Since the President now controls the Supreme Court, our only hope lies in influencing the members of Congress."

The historical evidence suggests the necessity for a thorough reevaluation of modern academic assumptions about Congress–Court relations. As far as Congressional attitudes were concerned, defense of the Supreme Court in 1937 was primarily a matter of political expediency rather than principled ideological commitment to the judicial institution. This contrasts with the conventional view. The conventional historical interpretation of the impact of the Court-packing fight consisted of three parts. First, the Supreme Court fight of 1937 spelled the beginning of the end for his [Roosevelt's] New Deal [Congressional] coalition." Second, out of the ashes of the Court Controversy was forged "a bipartisan anti-New Deal coalition."[3] The third, implicitly accepting the concept of widespread Congressional and public reverence for the Supreme Court, was the argument that "Congress and Country, which had been responsive to emergency measures, rejected the real motive of 'court-packing,' which was to ensure favorable opinions from the new justices to be appointed."[4]

[1] Senator Edward R. Burke, in foreword to Merlo J. Pusey, *The Supreme Court Crisis* (New York: Macmillan Co., 1937), p. vi.

[2] William E. Leuchtenberg, "Franklin D. Roosevelt's Supreme Court 'Packing' Plan," in Harold M. Hollingsworth and William F. Holmes, *Essays on the New Deal* (Austin: University of Texas Press, 1969), pp. 107–109.

[3] *Ibid.*, pp. 109 and 111.

[4] Broadus and Louise P. Mitchell, *A Biography of the Constitution of the United States: Its Origin, Formation, Adoption, Interpretation* (New York: Oxford University Press, 1964), p. 232.

The validity or invalidity of these interpretations of Congressional attitudes toward the Court and toward the New Deal are tested here by two approaches. The first embodies a thorough examination of conventional historical source material to determine factually the answers or at least clues to the resolution of the following interpretative questions. Did the Supreme Court controversy of 1937 serve as the most significant occasion for the development of an anti-New Deal conservative coalition? Or did such a coalition seize upon the Court crisis as a major opportunity to stop or slow the impetus of New Deal social and economic reform? Were the leading Congressional opponents of Roosevelt's Court plan traditional and consistent supporters of the Supreme Court? Did these opponents actually maintain a role as defenders of the Supreme Court after 1937 and especially after a "Roosevelt" majority controlled judicial decision-making?

The second approach comprises a comprehensive analysis of approximately 150 Court-oriented roll calls in the House and the Senate in the 79th through 90th Congress. If congressmen in general revere the Court, and lawyer-congressmen in particular possess, through professional socialization, an unusual sense of respect for the Supreme Court, it may be assumed that the variables which ordinarily influence congressional voting behavior would be considerably less efficacious when judicially-oriented legislation was being voted on than under other roll call circumstances. Do lawyer-congressmen deviate from their "normal" voting behavior patterns to consistently defend the Court? Do Congressmen abandon their partisan voting tendencies when Court-oriented legislation is acted upon? Do Congressmen who ordinarily oppose or support the conservative coalition continue to do so when legislation relating to the Supreme Court is before the House or Senate?

Both approaches may serve to identify some of the realities of modern Congress–Court relations.

DID THE COURT PACKING FIGHT SPAWN THE CONGRESSIONAL CONSERVATIVE COALITION?

Several key issues heralded the emergence of an anti-New Deal Conservative Coalition *before* the controversy over the Court-packing plan of 1937 arose. In 1935, bitter divisions resulted from the "death-sentence" clause of the Utility Holding Company Bill and from the "Wealth Tax" provisions of tax reform legislation. Commenting upon the impact of the Utility fight upon one group of hitherto loyal New Deal senators, historian James Patterson observed that "for all of them the 'death sentence' provision proved to be the expressed beginning of sustained opposition to the New Deal. In later years they would seek a conservative coalition."[5] He also noted that in connection with the 1935 Utility Holding Company "death sentence" issue, the new chairman of the House Rules committee, Congressman John O'Connor of New York devised a conservative strategy which was destined to be invoked often in subsequent years by refusing to grant a rule for action on the desired legislation.[6] When Roosevelt bypassed the committee and eventually got action in the Committee of the Whole House, he suffered a 224–152 vote defeat by teller note. The following day, the full House defeated Roosevelt's version of the Utility bill by a record vote of 258–147 and then substituted the weaker House version by the lopsided margin of 323–81. Patterson contended that

> The key 258–147 vote revealed the existence—for the first time since the New Deal began—of a conservative coalition in the House.[7]

The tax bill also roused formidable bipartisan opposition, as did legislation regulating the coal industry. Conservative opposition forced compromises which weakened the "tax the wealthy" emphasis of the original version.[8] The tax bill and utilities legislation controversies established the emergence of a conservative coalition of Southern Democrats and Northern Republicans in 1935, two years before the Court-packing controversy occurred.

It is very probable that the Court-packing fight of 1937, rather than marking the beginning of a Congressional anti-New Deal conservative coalition, provided an exceptional occasion for those members of Congress who sought a politically feasible opportunity to expand the anti-New Deal gains of 1935. Obviously there were, in addition, some members of Congress who were swayed adversely by

[5] James T. Patterson, *Congressional Conservatism and the New Deal* (Lexington: University of Kentucky Press, 1967), pp. 32–42.

[6] *Ibid.*, p. 53.

[7] *Ibid.*, p. 55.

[8] *Ibid.*, pp. 32–76.

the contents and proposed mode of adoption (statutory rather than amendatory) of the Court plan. But the public-policy positions and roll-call positions taken both *before* and *after* the Court fight of 1937 indicate that reverence for the Court or the federal judiciary was not a consistent motivation for most House and Senate members.[9] Patterson's research established that

> Within two months following introduction of the [Court] Plan, every Democratic Senator . . . whose dissatisfaction with the New Deal had already been apparent in late 1935 was also an open opponent of the court plan.[10]

Conceding that the Court-packing controversy was "the most damaging single blow to Roosevelt's senatorial coalition," Patterson nevertheless concluded that,

> The controversies in 1937 over such issues as relief spending, labor unions, and urban welfare programs indicate that Roosevelt would have encountered considerable conservative opposition in the 1937 session, court plan or not.[11]

WERE THE COURT-PACKING OPPONENTS CONSISTENT COURT SUPPORTERS?

One of the greatest ironies of the entire Court-packing controversy was the identity of the unwitting originator of the idea of reform by statutory replacement of superannuated judges—James Clark McReynolds, who had devised the plan for circuit and district judges while serving as Attorney General under President Woodrow Wilson.[12]

Similarly, the crucial leadership role of Senator Burton K. Wheeler in guiding opposition to the Court-packing plan elicited the plaintive comment from Frank Walker, a Roosevelt confidant, that

> . . . to find Burt in the front ranks of those who were piously upholding the sanctity of the Supreme Court . . . well, that was a sight to make the angels weep.[13]

[9] See Patterson, *ibid.*, pp. 77–84, for an account of private Congressional conservative planning and attitudes *before* the Court-packing controversy arose.

[10] *Ibid.*, p. 99.

[11] *Ibid.*, p. 128.

[12] Leuchtenburg, *op. cit.*, p. 74.

[13] *Ibid.*, p. 113.

Walker, like numbers of other political leaders of the 1930s, recalled that Wheeler, as Robert La Follette, Jr.'s vice-presidential running mate, had advocated limiting the Supreme Court's power in 1924.[14] Indeed, those Republicans who had previously been critical of the Court became determined opponents of Roosevelt's plan. It is clear that the Court-packing controversy served to coalesce congressional opposition against the New Deal despite the earlier anti-Court records of some of its 1937 defenders.[15]

The emergent Conservative Coalition gained considerable strength as a result of the 1938 congressional elections, both in sheer numbers and through conservative Democratic dissatisfaction resulting from Roosevelt's "purge" attempts in several Democratic senatorial primaries. In 1939, three major roll calls are identified by Patterson as the most significant illustrations of conservative coalition strength in the House: (a) the opposition to the New Deal "self-liquidating" projects legislation, 193–167; (b) the authorization for the investigation of the National Labor Relations Board, 254–134; and (c) the defeat of a New Deal housing bill, 191–178.[16] Although these issues were essentially economic, the beginning of a shift in the attitudes of congressional supporters of the Supreme Court in the Court-packing fight in 1937 could be detected. Howard Smith of Virginia, an influential member (later chairman) of the House Rules Committee, commented while supporting the investigation of the NLRB that,

> I voted against the National Labor Relations Board [in 1935] and I did so on the grounds that it was unconstitutional. I think it was palpably unconstitutional at that time. . . . But time has changed the Supreme Court and the Supreme Court has changed the Constitution.[17]

In the Senate, the successful invocation of senatorial courtesy by Senators Carter Glass and Harry Flood Byrd resulted in the overwhelming 72–9 vote against Roosevelt's nominee for a federal district judgeship in Virginia—Floyd Roberts.[18] By 1939, Roosevelt appointees comprised a majority on the Supreme Court, and the New Deal had gained strength through numerous inferior court appointments. Many conservative members of the House and Senate, therefore,

[14] Patterson, *op. cit.*, p. 115.
[15] *Ibid.*, pp. 85–125.
[16] *Ibid.*, p. 322.
[17] *Ibid.*, p. 317.
[18] *Ibid.*, p. 298.

were considerably less impressed by the call for reverence for the Supreme Court in 1939, despite their highly vocal support for the Court in the Court-packing controversy in 1937.

Conversely, a number of ardent supporters of Roosevelt's Court plan in 1937 became strong supporters of the Supreme Court in the 1940s. Senator Alben Barkley had been in the front rank of Roosevelt's supporters against the Court in 1937. By 1946, when conservative attacks upon the Court began to mount after the war years had diverted attention from domestic issues, Barkley emerged as one of the Supreme Court's most consistent supporters. Barkley's comments in Senate debate on Tidelands Oil legislation in July, 1946, touched indirectly upon the variety of economic forces seeking Congressional renewals of statutory interpretations.[19] Barkley continued to attack special interests in subsequent years, arguing in 1947 that,

> At the outset I wish to say I deplore the tendency of recent years either by legislation to anticipate decisions of the court and thereby in advance nullify them or make them impossible or irrelevant by the passage of legislation to nullify decisions after they have been rendered. That tendency has taken root in the Congress of the United States to a larger degree within recent years than in any previous time, so far as I can recall, in the history of the United States. We saw evidence of it two or three years ago in legislation designed to lift out of the purview and the scope of the antitrust laws insurance companies engaged in interstate commerce; as they were, and as they were declared later by the Supreme Court to be so engaged. Fortunately, through the members of the committee, among whom especially was the Senator from Wyoming, Mr. O'Mahoney, legislation was worked out which seemed to be satisfactory to the country and to all parties concerned. But the original proposal was a deliberate effort, Mr. President, to forestall an opinion of the Supreme Court with respect to certain rate practices. . . . It represents an effort to deny the Supreme Court of the United States the right to adjudicate litigation. . . . I therefore deplore this tendency of legislative interference with the functions and jurisdictions of the Courts.[20]

Arthur S. Miller has argued, building upon a seminal paper by Alan Westin, that Congress has developed a system of "appellate review" of administrative and judicial decisions which were viewed by business-oriented interest groups as detrimental. In a preliminary

[19] *Congressional Record*, 79th Congress, 2nd Session, July, 19, 1946, p. 9422.
[20] *Congressional Record*, 80th Congress, 1st Session, March 21, 1947, p. 2349.

survey of congressional attitudes and reversals embodying developments from 1944 to 1961, Westin theorized that the "development of resort to this 'Congressional Court of Appeals' by the American corporate community as a central political tactic [averted] what otherwise might have been a direct clash between business and the Supreme Court between 1944–1960."[21] Subsequent analysis of Congressional roll-call behavior provides an opportunity to explore, at least in part, the validity of Westin's hypothesis. But there is little doubt that the tendency detected by Senator Barkley was a strong and consistent one. Westin argued that Congressional overrulings of statutory interpretations by the Supreme Court before 1944 were "sporadic and infrequent." By 1959 Congressman Wilbur Mills confided to committee witness Crawford Greenwalt, president of the DuPont Corporation, that "it seems that it is becoming more and more almost a full time job of the Congress to correct the Supreme Court's desire to legislate."

As a matter of fact, Congressional critics of the Court were neither reluctant to assume the role of legislative appellate judges nor deficient in developing a broad institutional rationale for such legislative assumption of interpretative responsibility, as the following exchange from a 1946 committee hearing illustrates. In answer to a union official's query and argument,

> Is it sound legislation and wise public policy for the Congress to sit in judgment retroactively upon the Supreme Court? . . . If Congress is converted into a place to retry cases which have been lost in the Supreme Court, people will come running to Congress to act as a super Supreme Court.

Senator Alexander Wiley promptly replied:

> What is being worked out here today is part of the mechanics of our constitutional system of checks and balances. . . . I need hardly point out to my colleagues that the founding fathers contemplated three strong and independent branches of government—legislative, judicial and executive—each of which was, insofar as possible, to tend to its own knitting. That means that the legislative branch, which is Congress, should do the legislating. When this delicate system of checks and balances is thrown out of balance, as

[21] Alan F. Westin, "Corporate Appeals to Congress from Supreme Court Rulings" (Paper presented to the American Political Science Association, 1962), p. 1.

> I believe it is [by the decision here] the very foundation of our Republic is endangered . . . and Congress must reverse the Court.[22]

It seems clear that after World War II, the disenchantment with the "new" Supreme Court which had manifested itself among several leading defenders of the Court against Roosevelt's Court-packing plan in 1937 became progressively deeper. It also became broader by extension to new members of Congress who, because of ideological inclination or perceived constituency predilection, became successors to the original Conservative Coalition members of the 1930s. Ultimately, however, the identification of the attributes of Congressional behavior toward the Supreme Court and the federal judiciary must be established upon bases broader and stronger than the rhetorical utterances of selected Congressional leaders. Roll-call votes are, in the words of Anderson and his associates, both "hard" and "public data."[23] "Like statistics on elections, they represent discrete acts, the fact of whose occurrence is not subject to dispute. They do not depend for their validity as data upon verbal reports of action or upon the impressions of fallible observers."[24]

CONGRESSIONAL ROLL CALLS RELATING TO THE SUPREME COURT, 1945–1968

One hundred and forty-seven House and Senate roll calls* were voted upon in the period 1945–1968, which comprised virtually every division relating to Congress–Supreme Court relations in the post-World War II era. We sorted the Congressional roll calls which delineated the boundaries of Congressional and Supreme Court authority into three categories. Type I are roll calls which directly related to the institutional role of the Supreme Court and the inferior federal tribunals (i.e., a "Court-packing" statute or the curtailment of the Court's appellate jurisdiction). Type 2 are roll calls which at-

[22] Quoted in Westin, "Corporate Appeals," *op. cit.*, pp. 4 and 5.

[23] Lee F. Anderson, Meredith W. Watts, Jr., and Allan R. Wilson, *Legislative Roll-Call Analysis* (Evanston: North Western University Press, 1966), p. 5.

[24] Cited in Anderson *et al.*, *op. cit.*, pp. 5 and 6, from David B. Truman, *The Congressional Party* (New York: John Wiley and Sons, Inc., 1959), p. 12.

* All are categorized and described chronologically in John R. Schmidhauser, Larry L. Berg, and Albert Melone, "The Impact of Judicial Decisions: New Dimensions in Supreme Court–Congressional Relations," *Washington University Law Quarterly* (Spring, 1971), 239–251.

tempted to reverse or alter specific public policy decisions (i.e., numerous reversals of statutory interpretations) but do not involve attempts to alter the basic institutional relationship of Congress and the Supreme Court. Type 3 are roll calls which involved Supreme Court nominations. Congressional roll-call and membership data from the Inter-University Consortium for Political Research, Ann Arbor, Michigan, were utilized.

If, as Alan Westlin suggested, direct institutional clashes between the corporate business community and the Supreme Court were averted because business interests developed resort to Congress to secure reversals of anti-business judicial statutory interpretations, then the incidence of direct institutional attacks upon the Supreme Court would bear an inverse correlation to the number of Congressional reversals of statutory interpretations by the Court. As the members of the Conservative Coalition in Congress generally are favorably oriented toward the interest groups representing the business community (i.e., U.S. Chamber of Commerce, the National Association of Manufacturers, and other groups operating through interest-group "summit" conferences such as Greenbrier[24a]), do members of this coalition attack the Court institutionally more frequently when statutory reversals decrease or vice versa?

The evidence from Table 7-1 neither supports nor contradicts Westin's hypothesis. Roll calls, by the very fact that they have been invoked in the legislative process, generally represent divisions which were not susceptible to resolution by negotiation or bargaining. In all categories of issues, specific legislative disagreements sometimes produced a large number of roll-call divisions. In the 79th Congress, for example, five of the six statutory-interpretation reversal roll calls involved variations on a single parliamentary theme, the Congressional attempt to substitute its interpretation for that of the Supreme Court regarding Tidelands Oil. Thus the actual number of contested bills (indicated in parenthesis) is considerably smaller in most Congresses than the roll-call divisions called for by the protagonists of competing positions. The proliferation of roll-call divisions is, at best, a crude indicator of intensity of conflict and perhaps parliamentary skill. Ultimately, it will be necessary to utilize the total universe of legislative actions in each successive Congress in order to test

[24a] For a full discussion of the summit conferences held by business-oriented interest groups at Greenbrier, West Virginia, see Donald R. Hall, *Cooperative Lobbying* (Tucson: University of Arizona Press, 1969), pp. 32–34, 188–212.

TABLE 7-1. *Incidence of Congressional roll calls and bills on (1) reversal of Supreme Court statutory interpretations and (2) direct attacks on the Supreme Court as an institution by Congress: 1945–1968.*

Congress	Number of Roll Calls (Number of Contested Bills in Parentheses)	
	Statutory reversals	Direct institutional attacks
79th	6 (2)	1 (1)
80th	8 (2)	0
81st	20 (5)	0
82nd	12 (2)	0
83rd	15 (2)	1 (1)
84th	9 (1)	0
85th	12 (4)	5 (1)
86th	12 (3)	3 (1)
87th	2 (2)	0
88th	3 (2)	8 (2)
89th	3 (1)	9 (3)
90th	9 (2)	5 (1)

accurately the validity of Westin's hypothesis. The diminishing number of economic roll-call divisions generally apparent in the chronological order of Congresses from 1945 to 1968 may well reflect the growing success of the corporate business community in overturning statutory interpretations *without* provoking the numerous roll-call divisions characteristic of the late 1940s and the 1950s. In 1966, for example, the 89th Congress, importuned by various interest groups including the American Bar Association, passed H.R. 11256, a bill relating to the priority of federal tax liens and levies. Although this bill overruled two Supreme Court decisions,[25] it was approved as Public Law 89–719 without a roll-call division in either the House or the Senate.[26]

DIRECT INSTITUTIONAL ATTACKS BY CONGRESS

In historical context, the Supreme Court has experienced a number of periods in which it was subjected to heavy institutional attacks.

[25] *U.S.* v. *White Beer Brewing Company*, 350 U.S. 1010 (1956), and *U.S.* v. *Bull Construction Company*, 355 U.S. 587 (1958).

[26] From the data gathered by Albert Melone for *The American Bar Association and Public Policy, 1947–1968* (Preliminary draft of a doctoral dissertation, Iowa City, Iowa, 1970).

Stuart Nagel categorized seven such high-frequency periods before 1960.[27] Utilizing roll-call data from the 80th through 90th Congresses (the 79th will be treated more intensively in the concluding portion of this chapter), we examined the voting behavior of congressmen and senators in the ten roll calls in the House of Representatives and the twenty-one roll calls in the Senate which were distinctly attacks on the Court as an institution. We categorized such roll calls in a manner similar to Harry Stumpf's definition:

> any Congressional bill having as its purpose or effect, either expressed or implied, an alteration in the structure or functioning of the Supreme Court as an institution within the context of legislative-judicial conflict.[28]

Such proposals may seek to alter the professional requirements of members, the size of the Court, certain Court procedures such as the number of votes necessary to decide a case, or the Court's jurisdiction. A bill also may have a dual objective, seeking to curb the Court as an institution and, at the same time, to reverse its decisions. The proposed Jenner-Butler legislation of the 1950s is an example of such a bill. In this investigation all such dual-purpose measures are classified as anti-Court or Court-curbing (Type 1).

The Constitution, in Article III, granted the Supreme Court appellate jurisdiction "with such Exceptions, and under such Regulations as the Congress shall make" over all cases within the judicial power of the United States.[29]

The Supreme Court from time to time has used language in its opinions suggesting that by virtue of the exceptions and regulations clause its appellate jurisdiction is subjected to unlimited Congressional control. Leonard Ratner has argued that if Congress has such authority, it could do the following:

> 1. Deprive the Supreme Court of appellate jurisdiction and abolish lower federal courts, thereby confining the judiciary of the

[27] Stuart S. Nagel, "Court-Curbing Periods in American History," *The Vanderbilt Law Review*, Vol. XVIII, No. 3 (June, 1965), pp. 926–27.

[28] Harry P. Stumpf, "Congressional Response to Supreme Court Rulings: The Interaction of Law and Politics," *Journal of Public Law*, Vol. 14, No. 2 (1965) p. 382.

[29] United States Constitution, Art. III, Section 2, quoted in Leonard G. Ratner, "Congressional Power over the Appellate Jurisdiction of the Supreme Court," *University of Pennsylvania Law Review*, Vol. 109, No. 2 (December, 1960), p. 157.

United States to a single court exercising original jurisdiction over cases affecting ambassadors, public ministers, and consuls, or in which a state is a party.

2. Deprive the Supreme Court of appellate jurisdiction and other federal courts of all jurisdiction over cases involving the validity, under the Constitution, of state statutes or the conduct of state officials, thereby leaving to the highest court of each state the final determination of such questions.

3. Deprive the Supreme Court of appellate jurisdiction over any case arising under the Constitution, laws, or treaties of the United States, thereby allowing the federal courts of appeals and the highest state courts to become, in their respective jurisdictions, the final interpreters of federal law.[30]

Recommendations for limitation of the Court's appellate jurisdiction have not been limited to Congressional critics. Philip Kurland, a frequent academic critic of the Warren Court, made a drastic jurisdictional recommendation shortly after Chief Justice Earl Warren indicated that he would step down as Chief Justice:

> I would think the time has come to limit its (Supreme Court) authority to the adjudication of Constitutional issues alone.[31]

Professor Kurland obviously believed that Congress possessed strong authority to act in regard to the Court's jurisdiction. Leonard Ratner, however, concluded that the "exceptions and regulations" clause did not give Congress power to negate the essential functions of the Supreme Court.[32] The academic arguments have proliferated. Yet, it is absolutely clear from the actions taken by the Congress during the 1950s and 1960s that a clear majority in the House and a near majority in the Senate on several occasions voted in a manner which indicated that a substantial number of members of Congress believe the authority not only exists but should be exercised.

Congress and the Warren Court: Battle Lines Drawn

Earl Warren was sworn in as Chief Justice of the U.S. Supreme Court on October 5, 1953. Relations between the Court and Congress from

[30] Ratner, *op. cit.*, p. 158.

[31] Philip B. Kurland, "Limit Supreme Court's Jurisdiction," *Los Angeles Times* (July 14, 1968), Sec. G, p. 7.

[32] Ratner, *op. cit.*, p. 203.

1945 to the time of Warren's appointment were as noted characterized by periodic guerrilla skirmishes rather than all-out warfare, although the Bricker amendment controversy had judicial as well as Presidential overtones. Relations began to deteriorate soon after Warren's appointment when the Court handed down decisions on some of the more sensitive issues of the time, such as the landmark decision on school segregation, *Brown* v. *Board of Education* in 1954.[33] An examination of the legislative conflict with the Court during the late 1950s and the 1960s must, however, take into consideration the buildup of tensions during the 1940s. As the *Congressional Quarterly* pointed out in its excellent analysis of the actions of the 85th Congress, resentment against Court rulings were expressed as far back as 1942, when in the *Cloverleaf case*, the Supreme Court invalidated an Alabama law regulating food cleanliness on the ground Congress had pre-empted exclusive jurisdiction by enacting the Pure Food and Drug Act.[34] Herman Pritchett cited *Hines* v. *Davidowitz* (1941) as an even earlier sore point with Court critics.[35] Furthermore, the Court's actions in the area of race relations during the 1940s had been severely criticized by Southern congressmen. As Harold Spaeth pointed out in his analysis of the Warren Court, "after 1937, the Court began to concern itself much more with the issue of the relationships between government and the individual—that is to say, with the issue of civil liberties."[36] On the issues of race and segregation, the Vinson Court (1946–1953) moved against such practices but, in the words of Herman Pritchett, "with a conscious effort to disturb earlier rulings as little as possible."[37] Even this pace set by the Court on racial matters was sufficient to antagonize the Southerners in the Congress.

That the Warren Court would come under severe attack was therefore not surprising, in view of decisions handed down during the Chief Justice's tenure. Theodore Mitau suggested that with respect

> to the outcomes of judicial decision-making there is no neutrality. In this process of accommodation of conflicting interests and

[33] *Brown* v. *Topeka*, 347 U.S. 483 (1954).

[34] "Proposals to Set Aside Court Decisions," *Congressional Quarterly Almanac, 1958*, Vol. 14, 1958, p. 289.

[35] Pritchett, *op. cit.*, p. 73.

[36] Harold J. Spaeth, *The Warren Court: Cases and Commentary* (San Francisco: Chandler Publishing Co., 1966), p. 12.

[37] C. Herman Pritchett, *The Political Offender and the Warren Court* (Boston: Boston University Press, 1958), p. 7.

> values, usually someone gains and someone loses. Broadly speaking, those who gained from the libertarian decisions of the last decade (1954–1964) were the poor, the ill-educated, the underprivileged and the underrepresented. Their legal victories necessarily entailed losses in privilege and power to many Americans who viewed these Constitutional developments with much apprehension and intense hostility.[38]

The range of Conservative Coalition charges against the Court was broad. Some critics believed the Court had upset precedents and was basing its decisions on sociological rather than legal principles in order to bar racial segregation. To others, the Warren Court was allegedly ignoring long-established constitutional relations between states and the federal government and incorrectly striking down state laws under the pre-emption doctrine. It was accused of intruding on Congress' right of investigation and charged with endangering the national security by rulings in the subversive activities cases.[39] As numerous laws pertaining to internal security enacted by Congress and most states during and after World War II (when Warren took office 44 states had anti-sedition laws) came under review, the anti-Court feelings in Congress and the states increased. Before the Court retreated somewhat on this issue during the 1958 term (in the Barenblatt decision, to cite one example), numerous bills were before the Congress to curb the Supreme Court and substantially alter its position in the American political system.

The critical response in Congress to Court rulings was not limited to cases involving the federal government. Decisions on the security issue which affected the states also brought down the wrath of Congress on the Court (*Pennsylvania* v. *Nelson* is a good example). As Clifford M. Lytle pointed out:[40]

> In many instances the sympathies of Congressmen are not discordant with those of the states. In view of this Congress can act as an effective conduit through which the states can articulate their

[38] G. Theodore Mitau, *Decade of Decision: The Supreme Court and the Constitutional Revolution 1954–1964* (New York: Charles Scribner's Sons, 1967), pp. 3 and 5.

[39] *Congressional Quarterly Almanac, 1958, op. cit.* This general discussion is drawn from "Proposals to Set Aside Court Decisions," pp. 287–297.

[40] Clifford M. Lytle, "Congressional Response to Supreme Court Decisions in the Aftermath of the School Segregation Cases," *Journal of Public Law*, Vol. 12, No. 2, 1963, p. 303.

> grievances. This is especially true with respect to those judicial decisions involving the states and their fight against communism.[40]

In August of 1958, the Chief Justices of thirty-six states issued a report expressing grave doubt whether we have a government of laws and not men.[41] The American Bar Association entered the fray in 1959 when one of its committees charged that the Warren Court's decisions facilitated the march of Communism.[42] Whereas the earlier decisions on racial questions had provoked opposition primarily from the South, the Court's rulings on subversives provoked the wrath of the conservative coalition of Southern Democrats and Northern conservatives, primarily Republican in political party affiliation.

The battle over Court-curbing legislation which ensued during the 85th Congress found various organized groups supporting the proposals. They included the American Farm Bureau Federation, Conference of 48 Governors, Attorney General's Association of 48 States, Small Business Association, the American Medical Association, and other groups normally associated with the conservative ideological position. Those supporting the Court were the AFL-CIO, the Railway Labor Executive Association, the Association of American Railroads, the National Association for the Advancement of Colored People, and other groups active in civil rights and civil liberties causes.[43] The American Bar Association endorsed a somewhat more limited anti-Court proposal dealing with state sedition laws. The alignment of interest groups on the roll calls and, for the most part, the division in the Congress resembled alignments on civil rights and social welfare legislation. Representative Earl J. Holland aptly described the situation during the floor debate on H.R. 3 when he stated:[44]

> The sponsors and supporters of this bill are those who fought the right to vote, desegregation, civil rights, and all labor and humane legislation which has been passed.

Although Holland's statement obviously did not apply to every senator and congressman supporting the series of bills considered, the following roll call analysis indicates it was not far off the mark.

[41] *Report of the Committee on Federal-State Relationships as Affected by Judicial Decisions* (Chicago: Conference of State Chief Justices, 1958).

[42] Alpheus T. Mason, "The Supreme Court Under Fire Again," *The Reporter*, September 24, 1964, p. 46.

[43] *Congressional Quarterly Almanac, 1958, op. cit.*, p. 292.

[44] *Ibid.*, p. 291.

Court-Curbing Roll Calls: The House of Representatives

The House of Representatives did not vote on a measure designed to curb the court until the second session of the 85th Congress in 1958, when it gave approval to H.R. 3. The measure has been described by Pritchett as a "drastic anti-Nelson bill." In fact, the measure did not merely restore the effectiveness of state sedition laws rendered unenforceable by the Nelson ruling, a goal which could have been accomplished simply by enacting Section 2 of the bill. This limited action had been proposed by Congressman Lindsay and rejected by the House. H.R. 3 also was designed, by its statement of general principles, to govern and limit future Court decisions dealing with alleged conflict between federal and state laws.[45] The 86th Congress took three anti-Court roll calls, all successful for Court opponents; the 88th Congress voted twice on such measures, again with Court opponents succeeding; and the 89th Congress followed with two more roll calls, with the foes of the court in the majority on the substantive issue. During the period from 1958 to 1968, the House took a record vote a total of 10 times on anti-Court legislative proposals, with foes of the Court successful on 9 of the roll calls. Table 7-2 presents the division of the members of the parties on the 10 roll calls.

TABLE 7-2. *Average percentage of Democratic, Republican, and Northern and Southern Democratic representatives supporting the Court on roll calls directly attacking the Court or seeking to curb the Court.*

	Party			
	Dem.	Rep.	N. Dem.	S. Dem.
Average percentage (ten roll calls)	55.4	19.2	82.3	7.1

The most obvious conclusion which can be drawn from the table is that the three categories of partisans differ substantially in their voting behavior on the 10 anti-Court roll calls. The average percentage of Republican representatives supporting the Court is substantially lower than that of the Democrats. In direct contrast, a very high percentage (82.3%) of Northern Democrats were opposed to the anti-Court proposals. This percentage, compared to the average for the

[45] Pritchett, *op. cit.*, p. 81. The issue is discussed in Chapter 6, "The Preemption Issue," pp. 72–86.

entire Democratic Party, reflects the defection of a substantial number of Southern representatives from the position in support of the Court taken by the majority of Democratic representatives. On the 6 votes taken during the 85th and 86th Congresses, the largest number of Southern representatives supporting the Court on any given roll call was 2. Not one Southern representative in either Congress took a pro-Court position on the adoption of the rule for H.R. 3, and only two voted against the measure on final passage during the 85th Congress. The following year only one Southern representative opposed H.R. 3. The impact of this nearly unanimous opposition to the Court on the part of Southern representatives on the percentage of Democrats supporting the Court is obvious. There were between 60 and 85 Southerners taking an anti-Court position on the 6 roll calls during the two Congresses. On each occasion the defectors from the Southern position were from Texas. During the 85th Congress, Albert Thomas from Houston and Jack Brooks from the Beaumont-Port Arthur area supported the Court. Only Congressman Brooks did so the following year.

Representatives from the South were slightly more inclined to support the Court during the 88th Congress when 6 voted to accept the Rule on the Tuck Bill (H.R. 11926) pertaining to the Court's jurisdiction on reapportionment matters. There were 13 Southerners opposed to the anti-Court measure on final passage. Of the 6 voting against the rule, 2 were from Florida (Claude Pepper, Miami, and Sam M. Gibbons, Tampa), 1 was from Georgia (Charles Weltner, Atlanta), and 3 were from Texas (Albert Thomas, Houston; Henry Gonzalez, San Antonio; Robert Casey, Houston). On the vote dealing with reapportionment, all 6 members supporting the Court represented urban areas. Furthermore, most of these members supported the majority position of the Democratic Party far more frequently than the great majority of their Southern colleagues.

There were 13 representatives from the South opposing the Tuck measure on final passage. They represented districts in Virginia (2), Alabama (1), Florida (5), Georgia (1), Louisiana (1), and Texas (4). Once again, those members from the South supporting the Court represented urban areas such as Birmingham, New Orleans, and Fort Worth, or had overall voting records more closely approximating their colleagues from the north.

Examination of the 10 roll calls indicates that the lowest percentage (74%) of Northern Democratic support for the Court occurred during the first session of the 86th Congress when the House voted on the Rule (H.Res. 288) for H.R. 3, a bill to limit court application of the federal pre-emption doctrine and sponsored by Congressman Howard (Judge) Smith of Virginia. The percentage (7%) of Republicans supporting the Court also reaches its low point on this roll call. The Democrats approached their low point (45%) of the previous year as only 47% supported the Court on H.Res. 288. The inclusion of four roll calls involving votes on a House rule raises delicate questions as to whether these voting divisions actually indicate pro- or anti-Court positions. On the basis of Congressional debates on these rules, we deemed it appropriate to include these roll calls in the study. It is hypothesized that some members would support a rule to call up legislation regardless of the individual Congressman's substantive views on the measure; but, on the other hand, some pro-Court members who desire to avoid being on record substantively on the major policy issues may oppose a rule to escape a subsequent substantive roll call.

In numerous studies of Congressional roll-call behavior, the party variable has been a factor of great importance in most roll-call issue categories.[46] What is most significant about the 10 House Court-curbing roll calls is the symmetry maintained in the relationship between Court support positions of Northern Democrats, all Democrats, and Republicans as indicated in Figure 7-1. Summarizing the data, it is clear that the percentage of Republicans supporting the Court was substantially lower on every roll call. In contrast, over 50% of the Democrats in the House of Representatives supported the Court on 8 of the 10 roll calls. Over 75% of the Northern Democrats supported the Court on 9 roll calls. The significance of the distribution is clear when it is recalled that supporters of the Court failed to obtain majority approval for their position on 9 of the 10 votes. Their only success came in the 89th Congress on the vote on the rule on the Court pay-raise legislation. Supporters of Court during this Congress, characterized by most observers as the most "liberal" Congress in recent history and, by implication, presumably composed of more members likely to be sympathetic to many of the Court's decisions, were unable to defeat the attack on the Court. Only by a relatively small margin, 202–183, did they succeed in

[46] For an excellent discussion and summary of research findings see Malcom E. Jewell and Samuel C. Patterson, *The Legislative Process in the United States* (New York: Random House, 1966), pp. 416–435.

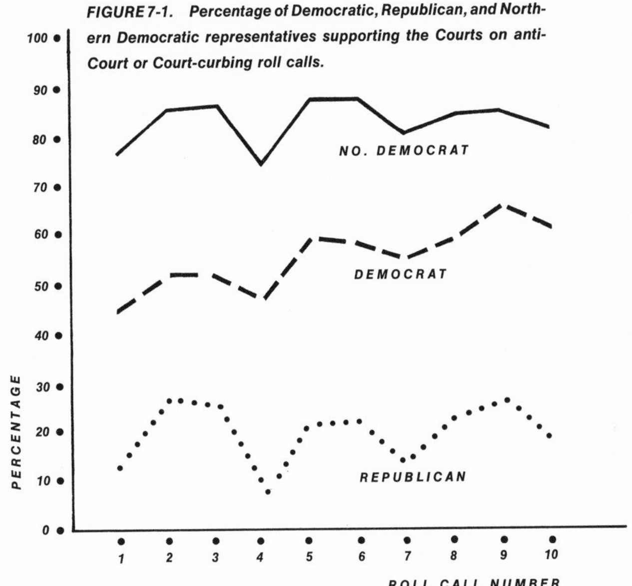

FIGURE 7-1. Percentage of Democratic, Republican, and Northern Democratic representatives supporting the Courts on anti-Court or Court-curbing roll calls.

bringing the pay-raise bill to the floor. It is interesting to note that despite the large number of Democrats in the 89th Congress (295), the Rule would have been defeated without the support of 19 Southern representatives (25.3% of the Southern bloc of 75 members actually voting on the measure). Of the 19 Southern Democrats supporting the Rule, 10 were from the state of Texas, 3 were from Florida and 2 were from Louisiana. No representatives from Mississippi, North Carolina, and South Carolina voted to support the rule, with one representative from each of the remaining Southern states voting with their Northern colleagues. On final passage 13 Southern members of the House or 18.1% of those voting (Texas, 7; Florida, 3; Louisiana , 1; Georgia, 1; Arkansas, 1) supported the pay increase for justices. The number and percentage of Southerners supporting the Court during the 89th Congress was considerably higher than previously. This increase is reflected in the fact that the percentage of all Democrats supporting the Court reached its highest level during the 89th Congress. In contrast, the number of Northern Democrats defecting from the position of the party majority reached its highest point on final passage of the pay bill.

TABLE 7-3. *Number of Republicans supporting the Court on anti-Court roll calls by Congress, session and geographical region.*

Congress and Roll Call No.	Region								
	NE	MA	ENC	WNC	Border	South	Mountain	Pacific	Total
85-2									
I	3	15	4	0	0	0	0	0	22
II	11	24	7	4	1	0	0	4	51
III	10	24	6	3	1	0	0	3	47
86-1									
I	2	6	0	1	0	0	0	0	9
II	4	18	2	1	1	0	0	4	30
III	4	17	3	2	1	0	0	3	30
88-2									
I	2	7	5	1	3	0	0	2	20
II	5	15	5	2	4	1	0	2	34
89-1									
I	4	13	9	3	1	0	0	3	33
II	4	7	7	1	1	0	0	3	23

The voting behavior of the Republican Party on the 10 roll calls does not suggest any pattern of changing attitudes toward Court-curbing legislation. However, an examination of those Republicans supporting the Court indicates that on each of the 10 roll calls the Court received a substantially greater degree of support from the eastern wing of the Republican Party. Representatives from the Mid-Atlantic and New England States provided over 50% of the Republicans supporting the Court on 7 of the 10 roll calls, exceeded 40% on 2, and accounted for over 30% on the remaining roll call. In direct contrast, not a single Republican congressman from the Mountain-state region supported the Court on any of the 10 roll calls.

The regional distribution of Republican support for the Court is shown in Table 7-3. Table 7-3 indicates clearly that Republican members of the House of Representatives outside the three eastern regions provided little support for the Supreme Court on the Court-curbing roll calls. In fact, a higher percentage of Southern congressmen supported the Court on the roll calls during the 88th and 89th Congress than of Republican representatives from all the states west of the Mississippi River. During the 89th Congress 25.3% of the Southerners supported the Rule on the pay raise bill while only 26.2% of *all* Republican members of the House of Representatives did so. On the vote on final passage 18.1% of the Southern Democratic members voted for the bill, as did 18.1% of the Republican representatives.

As can be anticipated from the previous discussion of the voting behavior of Southern Democratic representatives, the Democrats in the House of Representatives had by far the lowest index of cohesion on the 10 roll calls.[47] The average Rice Index of Cohesion for Democrats was only 14.0. This is a direct contrast to the 62.0 average for the Republicans and the 64.6 average for Northern Democrats. The index for the groups on each roll call is presented in Figure 7-2.

The Republicans were least united during the 85th Congress and most united during the 88th, whereas the Democrats were badly divided in all sessions, with their greatest unity during the 89th Congress. In the latter the unity achieved resulted when an abnormally high number of Southerners voted with their Northern colleagues.

[47] Lewis A. Froman, Jr., *The Congressional Process: Strategies, Rules, and Procedures* (Boston: Little, Brown and Company, 1967), p. 67. For a discussion of the Rice Index of Cohesion see Lee F. Anderson *et al.*, *Legislative Roll Call Analysis* (Evanston: Northwestern University Press, 1966), pp. 32–35.

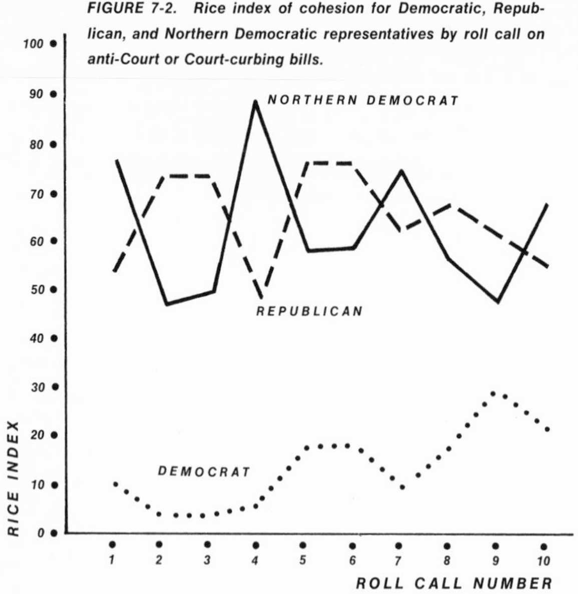

FIGURE 7-2. Rice index of cohesion for Democratic, Republican, and Northern Democratic representatives by roll call on anti-Court or Court-curbing bills.

The dissatisfaction with the United States Supreme Court which is so vividly recorded in the roll calls during the period under investigation leads one to speculate on just how many Democrats would have been needed in the House of Representatives to offset the nearly united opposition to the Court of conservative Republicans and Southern Democrats. Mayhew's study of the 1947–1962 period revealed that the number needed to enact modest programs in housing during the period against similarly united conservative opposition was in excess of 260.[48] Such majorities were present only during the 86th (282), the 87th (263) and the 89th (295), although there were 258 Democratic members during the 88th Congress.[49] More important for our purposes is Mayhew's observation that the "breaking-point on the thornier labor questions—minimum wage and labor-management relations—lay well above the 280 mark." With the exception of the 86th and the 89th Congress, such margins did not exist. The point can be made on the basis of

[48] David R. Mayhew, *Party Loyalty Among Congressmen: The Difference Between Democrats and Republicans, 1947–1962* (Cambridge: Harvard University Press, 1966), p. 114.

[49] Congressional Quarterly, *Politics in America: 1945–1966*. 2nd edition (Washington, D.C.: Congressional Quarterly Service, 1967, p. 96.

these votes, which appear to have stimulated deep ideological feelings on the part of the members of the House, that an even higher number may be required. As Mayhew pointed out:

> It is worthy of note that 322 Democrats were elected to the Congress that passed the Wagner Act in 1935, and that 333 Democratic Representatives sat in the Congress that enacted—narrowly—the Fair Labor Standards Act in 1938.[50]

It is clear that in the House of Representatives, 295 Democrats were not sufficient to defeat the Southern Democrat-Republican coalition which clearly carried the day on the Supreme Court pay-raise issue during the 89th Congress. The strong Republican support for Court-curbing measures is not surprising in view of the fact that on H.R. 3 the House Republican Policy Committee backed the measure. Pritchett noted that

> Perhaps the only incident in this long struggle which would dramatize the party division more starkly was the vote on the Jenner-Butler bill in 1958, which saw the Democratic Majority Leader, a Texan, Lyndon Johnson, voting to uphold the Court while the Republican minority leader, a Californian, Senator Knowland, joined its attackers.

Although the comment concerned the Senate it also is most appropriate for the House of Representatives, where even such a conservative Democrat as Francis Walter, Chairman of the House Committee on Un-American Activities, whose record as an "anti-communist" in the House could hardly be challenged by those similarly inclined, opposed H.R. 3. He did so because, as Pritchett pointed out, its backers had been unable to explain what it meant, what it would do, or why it was necessary.[51] The Republican voting record for the entire period under study indicates little change in attitude from the struggle over H.R. 3 during the 85th Congress to the battle to raise the pay for Court justices during the 89th Congress. In fact, in terms of actual numbers voting to support the Court, the opposition was even more intense. With the continued support of Southern Democrats and Republicans, sponsors of Court-curbing legislation will continue to be successful. Only the more restrained attitude of members of the Senate, aided by that institution's rules, prevented the measures discussed in this analysis from becoming law.

[50] Mayhew, *op. cit.*, p. 167.
[51] Pritchett, *Congress versus the Supreme Court*, *op. cit.*, pp. 127–28.

Direct Attacks on the Supreme Court in the Senate

There were 21 roll calls in the U.S. Senate during the period from 1947 through 1968 which were anti-Court or Court-curbing by nature. In addition to those measures voted on during the 85th Congress which were similar to the proposals considered by the House, the Senate took floor action on several measures which never came to the floor of the House of Representatives. For example, roll calls were taken on legislative proposals limiting court jurisdiction in the field of civil rights, voluntary prayers in public schools, the rights of defendants in criminal proceedings, and reapportionment. In addition to the broader range of issues considered in the Senate, a substantially larger number of amendments to the various measures were voted on during the period, a development similar to the findings of Clausen and Cheney in their recent analysis of Senate-House voting behavior on economic and welfare issues. In all of these issue categories, the Senate normally takes more roll calls than does the House and entertains a greater variety of amendments.[52] The Senate voted on 7 occasions on Court-curbing legislation related to reapportionment, 4 on crime, and 3 on the subject of voluntary prayers. Of the remaining roll calls, 2 were on the pre-emption question, 2 on civil rights, and 1 each on Fortas, judicial pay, and Congressional authority over Court jurisdiction.

The first occasion for the Senate to consider involving the Supreme Court as an institution came during the second session of the 83rd Congress (1954). In that session the Senate voted on a measure, Senate Joint Resolution 44, which would have amended the Constitution in the composition and jurisdiction of the Supreme Court. The resolution can only be understood in the context of Republican and Southern Democratic Congressional reactions to President Truman's role in the steel seizure controversy. The proposed amendment sought to take away Congressional authority to alter the Court's size and its appellate jurisdiction insofar as cases involving constitutional law were concerned. The measure was "pro-Court" in objective. It was especially significant because it provided a special opportunity to test the impact of a unique partisan effort which contradicted the "normal" pattern of voting on court-curbing measures. In striking contrast to virtually every other House or Senate

[52] Aage R. Clausen and Richard B. Cheney, "A Comparative Analysis of Senate-House Voting on Economic and Welfare Policy, 1953–1964," *The American Political Science Review*, Vol. LXIV, No. 1, March 1970, p. 141.

test of Court-related voting behavior, 100% of the Republican senators supported the pro-Court measure with only 44.4% of the Democrats doing so. Furthermore, 71% of the Northern Democrats opposed the pro-Court position.

This resolution, which has been described as an "indication of pleasure at the Court's preference of congressional over presidential authority" in the steel seizure case,[53] is unique among the 21 Senate roll calls included in this analysis. It is the only occasion when an overwhelming proportion of the Northern Democrats chose to withhold their support.

The remaining 20 roll calls included in this analysis indicated voting alignments more similar to the House. Legislation such as the Jenner-Butler bill (S2646), which would have limited appellate jurisdiction of the Court, was readily classifiable as anti-Court or Court-curbing. Although none of the far-reaching measures approved by the House became law, the narrow margin of their defeat in the Senate on several occasions and the necessity for Senate supporters of the Court to use the institution's rules on "extended debate" to achieve success clearly indicated the severity of the critical attitude toward the Warren Court on the part of a substantial group of senators.

TABLE 7-4. *The average percentage of Democratic, Republican, and Northern and Southern Democratic senators supporting the Supreme Court on roll calls on legislation to curb or directly attack the Court.*

	Party			
	Dem.	Rep.	N. Dem.	S. Dem.
Average percentage (21 roll calls)	60.0	37.3	83.0	15.2

The partisan divisions in the Senate on Court-curbing proposals during the period under study is somewhat similar to the pattern presented previously for the House of Representatives. Table 7-4 illustrates the voting pattern for all twenty-one roll calls.

Table 7-4 shows that although the average percentage of Republican senators supporting the Court (37.3%) is considerably higher than was the case in the House of Representatives (19.6%), it remains substantially below the level of support for the Court

[53] Murphy, *op. cit.*, p. 78.

provided by the Democrats (60.0%). The differences are more pronounced if the first roll call on S. J. Res. 44 is removed from the tabulations. The average percentage of Democrats supporting the Court in the Senate is somewhat higher than was the case in the House, 60.0% as opposed to 55.4% ,whereas the percentage for House and Senate Northern Democrats is nearly identical, 83.0% for the Senate and 82.3% for the House. Most significantly, the more urban-based Senate demonstrated stronger support for the Court in every partisan category.

Examination of the individual roll calls indicates that on 3 of the roll calls, a higher percentage of Republicans than Democrats supported the Court. In addition to S. J. Res. 44, such was the case during the 88th Congress when the Senate voted on an anti-Court amendment to the 1964 Civil Rights Act. On the roll call 80% of the Republicans, 71% of the Democrats, and 96% of the Northern Democrats opposed the amendment. The anti-Court Amendment had originated with Southern Democrats, who provided 16 of the 24 favorable votes. The Southerners were joined by 2 Democratic Senators from border states and 6 Republicans.[54]

The third occasion on which a higher percentage of Republicans than Democrats took a pro-Court position also was in the 88th Congress when Senator Strom Thurmond of South Carolina sponsored an amendment to the Dirksen proposal on reapportionment. Senator Thurmond attempted to offer as a substitute H.R. 11926, or the "Tuck Bill" as it was known in the House of Representatives. The bill would have withdrawn jurisdiction of federal courts over pending and future cases involving state legislative apportionment. Professor Gordon Baker had pointed out that "so drastic a statute had not been passed since Congress denied the Supreme Court appellate jurisdiction over the Reconstruction Acts after the Civil War."[55] Once again Southern Senators provided most of the support with 16 votes, along with a single Border-State senator and 4 Republicans.

[54] The regional breakdown for this analysis is that of the Inter-University Consortium for Political Research, University of Michigan. The border states are Kentucky, Maryland, Oklahoma, Tennessee, and West Virginia. The Southern states include Alabama, Arkansas, Georgia, Florida, Louisiana, Mississippi, North Carolina, South Carolina, Texas, and Virginia. The term Northern Democrat refers to Democratic Senators in all states outside the 10-state Southern region.

[55] Gordon E. Baker, *The Reapportionment Revolution* (New York: Random House, 1966), pp. 135–136.

The 2 votes on which the Republican percentage supporting the pro-Court position exceeded that of the Democrats. Both involved most severe measures originating with Southern senators. In each instance the Conservative Coalition lacked solidarity. On each of the remaining roll calls, the percentage of the Republicans supporting the Court was lower than that of the Democrats and, on several occasions, very substantially lower. With the exception of the vote on S. J. Res. 44, the Republican percentage of Court support never exceeded that of the Northern Democrats.

The percentage of Democrats taking a pro-Court position did not fall below 50% after the vote on S. J. Res. 44 during the 83rd Congress. The lowest level of support was reached during the 88th Congress on the vote on an amendment by Senator Gordon Allott which reduced the pay raise for Supreme Court Justices from $7,500 to $4,500. The amendment, which was approved, was opposed by only 29 of the 57 Democrats voting, or 51%. Similarly, the percentage of Northern Democrats voting in support of the Court also reached its lowest point on the pay-raise measure. Of the 38 Democrats supporting the Allott anti-Court Amendment, 14 were from the South. However, the remaining 14 senators voting against the Court represented states in most geographical regions. The only exceptions were the Pacific states and the Mid-Atlantic area where no opposition to the Court was found.[56] As was true one year later in the House of Representatives, the pay-raise issue provided a convenient means by which members of the Senate could express dissatisfaction with the Court and its decisions for the benefit of their constituents without actually altering the jurisdiction or make-up of the Court.

The average percentage of each of the three groups supporting the Court during a single Congress reached its lowest point during the 89th Congress. There was a substantial drop in support for the Court, particularly among Republicans, where the percentage did not exceed 10% on any of the six roll calls. Discussing the Court's actions preceding this Congress, Walter Murphy pointed out that the Court had dealt with 64 cases involving civil liberties, with 56 (87%) decided in favor of the claimant.[57] The Court had also acted on such controversial matters as one man, one vote, had again struck down

[56] The Pacific States include California, Oregon, and Washington; and the Mid-Atlantic states are Delaware, New Jersey, New York, and Pennsylvania.

[57] Walter F. Murphy, "Deeds Under a Doctrine: Civil Liberties in the 1963 Term," *American Political Science Review*, Vol. LIX, No. 1, March, 1965, p. 69.

officially sanctioned prayers, had laid down new principles in the field of criminal law, and had invalidated two acts of Congress. Murphy observed:

> Most immediately, the Justices once again found themselves embroiled in political controversy, their decisions attacked by the Republican party platform, by the Republican Presidential candidate, and by many members of Congress.[58]

An examination of the roll calls during the 89th Congress clearly revealed the displeasure of Republican senators with the Court's rulings on prayers and reapportionment. The largest number of Republican senators supporting the Court on any of the 6 roll calls was 3. On each of the roll calls pertaining to reapportionment, the three senators supporting the Court represented states located in the Mid-Atlantic region of the United States (Senators Boggs, Delaware; Javits, New York; Case, New Jersey).

The negative attitude toward the Court by Republican senators during the 88th and 89th Congress, as reflected in their voting behavior on proposals to curb the Court, was consistent with the general attitude of the party on the issue of reapportionment as expressed in the 1964 Republican national platform. Professor Gordon Baker described the platform provision as an effort to undercut the full effect of the Court's ruling by pledging "support of a constitutional amendment . . . enabling states having bicameral legislatures to apportion one house on bases of their choosing, including factors other than population."[59]

During the course of the 1964 Presidential campaign, the Republican nominee, Senator Barry Goldwater frequently criticized the Supreme Court for many of its rulings, including those on reapportionment.[60] The Republican nominee, according to Walter Murphy and Joseph Tanenhaus, formally opened his attack on the Supreme Court in an address before the American Political Science Association on September 11, 1964.

> The case of his indictment was that the Court had played a vital part in diminishing the freedom of state officials to handle local problems. He charged that of the three branches of the national government "today's Supreme Court is least faithful to the con-

[58] *Ibid.*, p. 64.
[59] Baker, *op. cit.*, p. 135.
[60] *Ibid.*

stitutional tradition of limited government." He singled out for special condemnation the Court's decisions holding prayers in public schools to be unconstitutional, and ordering reapportionment of state and congressional legislative districts to conform to the doctrine of "one man, one vote." These decisions, Goldwater alleged, reflected personal value preferences rather than legitimate interpretations of the Constitution. As such they were exercises of "raw and naked power."[61]

Senator Goldwater had also criticized Court decisions that had broadened the procedural safeguards to which those suspected of criminal conduct were constitutionally entitled and charged the Court with contributing to the breakdown of law and order "just to give criminals a sporting chance to go free." With attacks on the Court regularly made by the party standard-bearer, Barry Goldwater, the minority leader of the Senate, Senator Everett Dirksen, and a number of other Republican leaders in the Congress, the voting behavior of Republican senators on reapportionment and school prayers may be interpreted as consistent with the Party's acknowledged position.

The Democrats were divided on the issues of reapportionment and voluntary school prayers. The party's 1964 platform remained silent on the matter of reapportionment and, "although the Court was not totally without defenders, President Lyndon Johnson was not among the more vocal." The President, according to Tanenhaus and Murphy, said nothing at all either in defense of the Court or in criticism of Goldwater for seeking to profit by injecting the Court into the campaign. Although the nature of the 1964 campaign and President Johnson's desire to avoid controversy may have been correct in terms of the shortrun maximization of votes, it contributed little to the defense of Court and its decisions. In fact, when asked at a press conference in September if he had any views on the Dirksen–Mansfield proposal on reapportionment, President Johnson had answered: "No, sir."[62]

The interest-group line-up on the reapportionment controversy did not differ greatly from that of earlier battles over the Court (1958 and 1959), with groups that traditionally supported the conservative

[61] Walter F. Murphy and Joseph Tanenhaus, "Public Opinion and Supreme Court: The Goldwater Campaign," *Public Opinion Quarterly*, Vol. XXXII, No. 1, Spring, 1968, pp. 32–33.

[62] *Ibid.*, pp. 33–34.

position opposing the Court. The *Congressional Quarterly* reported that among those major organizations *actively* lobbying and working for the Dirksen Amendment were the ever-present American Farm Bureau Federation, the Chamber of Commerce of the U.S. and its constituent local groups, the National Association of Manufacturers and its local groups, the American Retail Federation, and various groups of state officials, primarily legislators. The groups opposing the amendment included the AFL-CIO and constituent unions, the American Civil Liberties Union, Americans for Democratic Action, an amalgam of liberal organizations called the National Committee for Fair Representation and, at a later date, the Leadership Conference on Civil Rights.[63] The line-up did not differ significantly from that found on civil rights and social welfare issues during the late 1950s and the 1960s. Indeed the battle over the Supreme Court during the mid-sixties differed little in terms of group support and voting alignment from battles over social, economic, welfare, and civil rights legislation.

The most severe Court-curbing proposals were defeated in the Senate. In addition to the Tuck proposal offered by Senator Thurmond, far-reaching and patently unconstitutional proposals limiting the jurisdiction of the federal courts were eliminated from the 1968 Omnibus Crime Control and Safe Streets Act, but only after tough parliamentary maneuvering. This measure, which the *Congressional Quarterly* labeled "the most extensive anti-crime legislation in the nation's history," contained in Section 2 some of the most far-reaching anti-Court proposals voted upon by the Senate in modern times.[64] Richard Harris described Title II as constituting "the most sweeping attack on the Supreme Court since Franklin Roosevelt tried to expand its membership in 1937." Francis Allen, dean of the University of Michigan Law School, concluded that the new assault "may be a more insidious threat, for it is less forthright and candid, and its dangers less apparent to the public at large."[65]

The most extensive aspect of the bill, Title II purported to overturn a series of Supreme Court decisions dealing with confessions and eyewitnesses. The decisions affected were *Mallory* v. *U.S.* (1957),

[63] Congressional Quarterly, *Representation and Apportionment* (Washington, D.C.: Congressional Quarterly Service, 1966), pp. 30–32.

[64] Congressional Quarterly, *Crime and Justice in America* (Washington, D.C.: Congressional Quarterly Service, 1968), p. 40.

[65] Richard Harris, *The Fear of Crime* (New York: Frederick A. Praeger, 1969), pp. 58–59.

Miranda v. *Arizona* (1966), and *U.S.* v. *Wade* (1967). In the Mallory decision, which several Congressmen had sought to overturn or alter since 1958, the Court ruled that a police interrogation after arrest and prior to arraignment violated Rule 5(a) of the Federal Rules of Criminal Procedure that "arraignment be without unnecessary delay" and violated the Court's supervisory role, enunciated in *McNabb* v. *U.S.* (1943), that delay "must not be of a nature to give opportunity for the extraction of a confession."

The Court had ruled in Miranda that before interrogation police must advise a suspect that anything he said could be used against him and that he had the right to remain silent, to obtain a lawyer of his choice, and to have a lawyer appointed if he were indigent. If the procedures were not followed, it would be a violation of the individual's Fifth Amendment privilege against self-incrimination.

Finally, in *United States* v. *Wade* (1967), the Court held that identification based on police lineup in the absence of a lawyer, and having no independent origin beyond that, was inadmissible at a trial. The absence of a lawyer was a violation of the Sixth Amendment right to counsel.

Although we did not classify the roll calls on those provisions of Title II that sought to overturn these decisions as Court-curbing (Type 1), the issues have been summarized briefly in order to provide some background for the presentation of Senator Ervin's drastic Court-curbing proposals. These were added to Title II during committee consideration of the measure (S917). The Ervin amendments adopted by the Senate Judiciary Committee sought to deny jurisdiction to federal Courts with regard to voluntary confessions and eyewitness testimony. The Senator also gained committee approval of an amendment which would have prohibited the Supreme Court and lower federal courts from reviewing an individual's conviction in a state court on a writ of habeas corpus.[66] Of the three Court-curbing provisions in Title II, the last was the most drastic.

The floor debate on Title II was replete with severe attacks on Chief Justice Earl Warren and the contemporary Supreme Court. Senator McClellan's opening statement on the bill was a charge that the Supreme Court desired to "protect and liberate guilty and confirmed criminals to pursue and repeat their nefarious crimes." Senator Ervin added:

[66] Congressional Quarterly, *Crime and Justice in America*, *op. cit.*, pp. 40–41.

> I ask the Senator from Arkansas (McClellan) if he does not agree with the Senator from North Carolina that members of the Senate who believe that self-confessed murderers, rapists, robbers, arsonists, burglars and thieves ought to go unwhipped of justice ought to oppose this bill.

McClellan replied: "If I were in sympathy with the criminals, I would vote against the bill. . . ."

McClellan and his fellow Court critics received assistance from the man whom Richard Harris described as their "most eminent supporter"—Richard M. Nixon. Presidential candidate Nixon's first position paper on crime, entitled "Toward Freedom from Fear," accused the Supreme Court of "seriously hamstringing the peace forces" in favor of criminals and called for new laws to "redress the balance." If the Court knocked them down, Nixon called for a Constitutional amendment to the same end.[67] The Presidential candidate went on to charge that proper response to crime lay not in cleaning up the slums but in locking up more malefactors.

The Senate debated the measure for three weeks under circumstances which frequently made rational discussion of the far-reaching constitutional issues contained in the crime bill extremely difficult. Donald G. Morgan's caution on the danger of bringing up measures of dubious constitutionality during a pre-election session is most appropriate in this instance:

> recurrent crises have demonstrated that public excitement and party contentiousness may force measures of dubious constitutionality or wisdom onto the floor in the last hectic days of a pre-election session. At such times those seeking immediate political advantage may overleap all the hurdles which reason, experience, and tradition have put up to assure deliberation. At such times, too, members may secure passage of measures which later prove highly questionable, without full awareness of their true character.[68]

Although the 90th Congress was not approaching adjournment when it approved the Omnibus Crime Bill, it was rapidly approaching the two Presidential nominating conventions in a year of considerable political turmoil and in a highly charged atmosphere over

[67] Harris, *op. cit.*, pp. 72–73.

[68] Donald G. Morgan, *Congress and the Constitution: A Study of Responsibility* (Cambridge: The Belknap Press of Harvard University Press, 1966), pp. 344 and 360.

the war in Southeast Asia, law and order, and other issues. Harris' analysis and the level of debate in the *Congressional Record* underscore the validity of Morgan's view.

The Senate on May 21, 1968, took roll calls on three amendments by Senator Joseph Tydings deleting Senator Ervin's Court-curbing provisions. Although the Senate refused by a large margin (51–31) to strike Title II from the bill, it did agree to delete the language denying or limiting court jurisdiction in the areas of confessions, eyewitness testimony, and writs of habeas corpus. On each of the three roll calls, over 90% of the Northern Democrats (92%, 91%, 97% respectively) supported the pro-Court move by Tydings. Only three Northern Democratic Senators opposed the amendments dealing with confessions and eyewitness testimony. They were Senators Cannon of Nevada, Hayden of Arizona, and Byrd of West Virginia. On the vote to strike the provision dealing with habeas corpus, only Senator Carl Hayden opposed the amendment.

On the three roll calls the percentage of the Democratic Party supporting the Court was higher than its average for all 21 roll calls. The small number of Northern Democrats defecting from the majority position accounts for much of the percentage increase. There also were, however, three Democratic senators from the South (Fulbright, Yarborough, Spong) voting with their Northern colleagues, and above average support for the majority position came from senators representing border states.

The percentage of Republican senators supporting the Court on the three Court-curbing roll calls also was high—52%, 53%, 57%—with 16 Republicans supporting Tydings on the first 2 votes and 17 supporting him on the habeas corpus amendment.

As was true on the more severe Court-curbing roll calls discussed previously, those proposals originating in the South or from the Senate's more conservative Republicans were not able to gain a great deal of support. The intemperate nature of the debate and the tactics of the proponents of Court-curbing undoubtedly had some negative impact on Senate members. It must be emphasized, however, that on a vote to prohibit the federal judiciary from granting the writ of habeas corpus to prisoners who claimed that a state had unjustly locked them up, 43% of the Republicans and 27% of the Democrats supported a rather substantial limitation on the "great writ." Furthermore, on an effort to remove all of Title II, a section described as unconstitutional by several legal experts, Court supporters could round up only 23% of the Republicans, 47% of the Democrats, and 72% of the Northern Democrats. Furthermore, there was strong support for keeping the provisions of Title II that modified or reversed the Mallory, Miranda, and Wade decisions. Finally, on final passage of the McClellan bill only four Senators opposed the measure (Senators Metcalf, Fong, Hart, and Cooper).

The measure was approved by the House of Representatives by a vote of 368–17, with 48 members not voting. In the 90th Congress a majority was not quite willing to drastically alter the appellate jurisdiction of the Supreme Court, but a majority had few qualms about modifying Constitutionally-based rulings by passing statutory reversal bills.

The failure of the more severe anti-Court proposals in the Senate has been attributed to various factors, e.g., the prestige of the Court, a judicial retreat in the highly controversial areas, the alleged unwillingness of the Congress to upset the traditional concept of separation of powers, and the like. An examination of the cohesion of the partisan groupings in the Senate suggests that other factors also may be relevant to an understanding of the defeat of Court-curbing legislation.

FIGURE 7-3. Percentage of Democratic, Republican and Northern Democratic senators supporting the Supreme Court on anti-Court or Court-curbing roll calls.

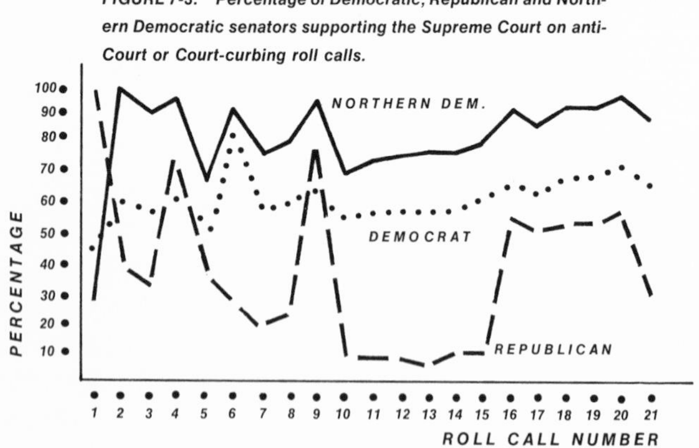

As in the House of Representatives, the Democrats were the least cohesive group of Senators. The average Rice Index of Cohesion for all 21 roll calls for the Democrats was 25.5. The indexes for the Republicans and Northern Democrats were 48.1 and 70.0 respectively. The cohesion indexes for the Senate Democrats and Northern Democrats are substantially higher than in the House of Representatives and, as was pointed out, the greater unity was found in support of the Court. Furthermore, the cohesion index of the Republican senators was considerably lower in the Senate. In fact, during the 90th Congress, when Ervin's drastic proposals were voted upon, the average Index of Cohesion for Republican senators on the six roll calls was a very low 11.7. On four of these roll calls the group was almost evenly divided. The average for the Northern Democrats was a high 83.6. The margin of victory for supporters of the Court is indicated clearly from the indexes.[69] There were 44 Northern Democrats and 36 Republicans in the Senate during the 90th Congress. The number of Northern Democrats in the Senate was relatively constant from the 86th Congress to the 90th, which meant that with fairly high cohesion on the part of Northern Democrats, it was very difficult for proponents of Court-curbing legislation to gain Senate approval and almost impossible if the measure was in the form of a constitutional amendment requiring a two-thirds majority. That this cohesion existed is clear from the previous discussion where it was pointed out that a majority of Democrats supported the Court on 20 of the 21 roll calls. Whenever the Republicans were divided on the issue, the 15 to 18 Southern foes of the Court who regularly supported all Court-curbing measures found it impossible to muster the remaining votes necessary for victory. Republican groups did not number over 36 senators after the 85th Congress and totaled only 32 during the 89th Congress and 33 during the 88th.

The fact that Court-curbing legislation failed in the Senate may be associated with the number of Northern Democratic senators. For example, during the battle over the Jenner-Butler bill in the 85th Congress, the Senate was evenly divided, with 49 Democrats and 47 Republicans. This legislation very nearly passed and, as Murphy so correctly pointed out, the leadership role of Majority Leader Lyndon Johnson was a major factor in its defeat. But why then did not the Senate Court opponents continue the battle during the following Congress, especially as the House had once again approved

[69] Complete graphic analysis of each roll call and specific identification of each roll call have been compiled in a preliminary article, John R. Schmidhauser, Larry L. Berg, and Albert Melone, "The Impact of Judicial Decisions: New Dimensions in Supreme Court-Congressional Relations, 1945–1969," *Washington University Law Quarterly* (Spring, 1971).

similar legislation? The literature suggests that a slight retreat on the part of the Court was crucial.[70] This may provide a partial explanation. However, an examination of the 1958 election returns may offer an additional clue. Whereas there were only 49 Democrats in the Senate during the 85th Congress when the Court-curbing proposals were narrowly defeated, there were 64 Democrats in the Senate during the 86th Congress. Furthermore, most of the Democratic gains were in northern industrial states, and virtually to a man, each new Democratic senator was a supporter of the Court. The new Democratic senators of the "class of '58" represented states such as Michigan, New Jersey, Ohio, California, Connecticut, Indiana, Maine, and Minnesota. It does not seem unreasonable to suggest that the electoral results contributed to the failure of Court opponents to bring this legislation to the floor.

This change in the partisan make-up of the Congress also may have contributed to the narrower margin of approval given Court-curbing legislation in the House of Representatives during the 86th Congress. In the 85th Congress there were 233 Democrats and 200 Republicans in the House, whereas in the 86th the division was 282 to 154. Furthermore, the Democratic gains in the House were in districts which had been represented by Republicans with a poor record of a support for the Court, notably from states such as Colorado, Kansas, Iowa, Minnesota, Nebraska, South Dakota Wisconsin, and Wyoming. The Republicans lost 23 seats in the 1958 election in the Midwest.[71] In short, opponents of the Court lost a sizeable number of allies as a result of the 1958 election. It is probably quite true that the Court's rulings in cases such as *Barenblatt* had the effect of cooling the demand and urgency for Court-curbing legislation. The partisan make-up of the Congress may be associated with the cooling-off experience. There simply were fewer opponents of the Court in the Congress after the 1958 election. A careful examination of the roll call votes in the House indicates that when the percentage of Northern Democrats increased, the margin of victory for Court opponents decreased.

The Republican members of the United States Senate during the 90th Congress differed substantially from their earlier colleagues with regard to voting behavior on Court-curbing legislation. Whereas

[70] Murphy, *Congress and the Supreme Court*, *op. cit.*, p. 249.

[71] The figures are drawn from the Congressional Quarterly volume entitled *Politics in America, 1945–1966*, cited previously, pp. 26–65.

Republican senators were quite united in their opposition to the Court during the 88th and 89th Congress, they were sharply divided on the matter during the 90th. With this assistance from Republicans, the Northern Democrats were able to form a majority capable of decisively defeating Ervin's proposals.

This analysis of Congress–Court relations in the area of Court-curbing legislation has emphasized partisan and regional divisions. Despite the strong academic contentions emphasizing the institutional prestige of the Supreme Court, this preliminary investigation of direct institutional attacks upon the Court raises serious questions about the validity of the "reverence" theme. In both the House and the Senate the patterns of partisan and regional voting divisions bear a marked resemblance to those relating to other issue categories. We will present an over-all appraisal of the significance of these findings at the conclusion of the subsequent section on Congressional voting behavior relating to reversals of statutory interpretations previously made by the Supreme Court.

CONGRESSIONAL REVERSAL OF STATUTORY INTERPRETATIONS

A number of students of the Supreme Court have argued that a discernible distinction can be made between Congressional attitudes toward the Court regarding ordinary legislative reversals of statutory interpretations and extraordinary actions which, in substance, would weaken the Court as an institution. Summarizing conventional historical descriptions of legislative anti-decision and anti-Court attacks, Stuart Nagel argued that "relatively milder" Court-curbing bills had a "substantially higher rate of success."[72] More specifically Harry Stumpf concluded that

> The prestige or sacrosanctity argument in Congress is used and used with some effectiveness in protecting the judiciary against anti-Court legislative reaction. . . . However, in anti-decision action, especially in simple reversals, the argument that reversal advocates are showing disrespect for the Court is not only little used, but if used at all, is almost totally ineffective.[73]

[72] Stuart S. Nagel, *The Legal Process from a Behavioral Perspective* (Homewood, Illinois: The Dorsey Press, 1969), p. 277.

[73] Harry F. Stumpf, "Congressional Response to Supreme Court Rulings: The Interaction of Law and Politics," *14 Journal of Public Law* (1965), p. 394.

Presumably, if Stumpf's hypothesis is correct, members of Congress may be expected to demonstrate higher levels of support for the Supreme Court when voting on roll calls involving direct institutional attacks on the Court than when the roll calls involve statutory reversals. Tables 7-5 through 7-8 and Figures 7-4 through 7-7 effectively sum up the analysis, with the results affirming Stumpf's hypothesis. In fact a comparison of the average percentage of Democratic, Republican, and Northern Democratic representatives supporting the Court in the 80th through 90th Congresses indicates stronger Court support in direct Court-curbing roll calls for every

FIGURE 7-4. Percentage of Democratic, Republican, and Northern Democratic representatives supporting the Supreme Court on roll calls to modify or reverse Court decisions.

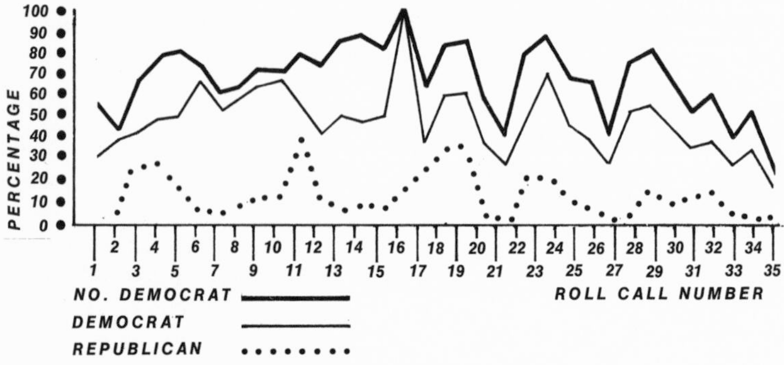

FIGURE 7-5. Rice Index of Cohesion for Democratic, Republican, and Northern Democratic representatives on roll calls to reverse or modify Supreme Court decisions.

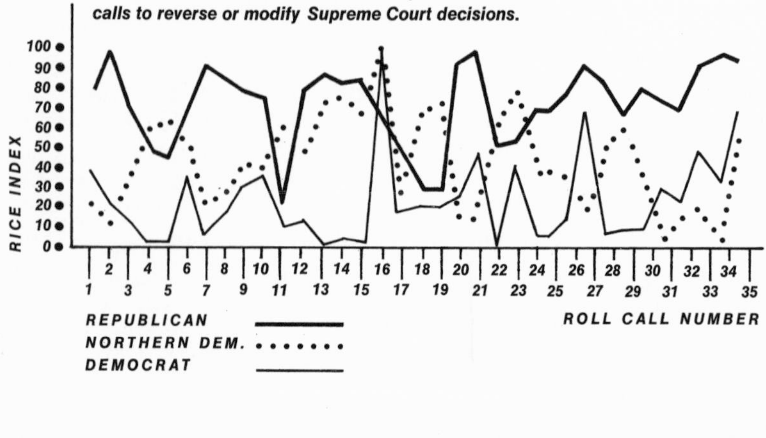

RICE INDEX

ROLL CALL NUMBER

REPUBLICAN

NORTHERN DEM.

DEMOCRAT

FIGURE 7-6. Percentage of Democratic, Republican, and Northern Democratic senators supporting the Supreme Court on roll calls to modify or reverse Court decisions (71 roll calls).

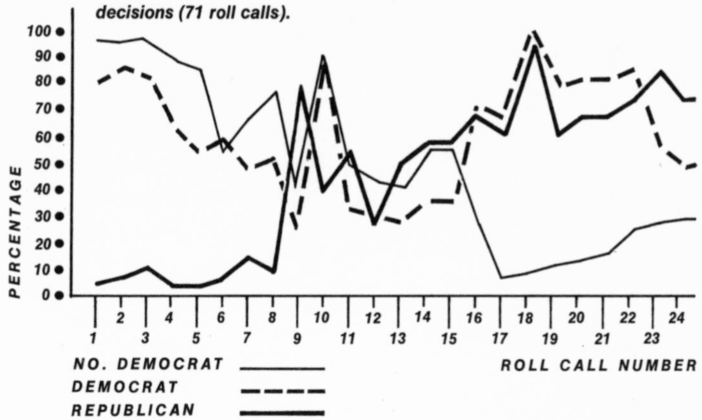

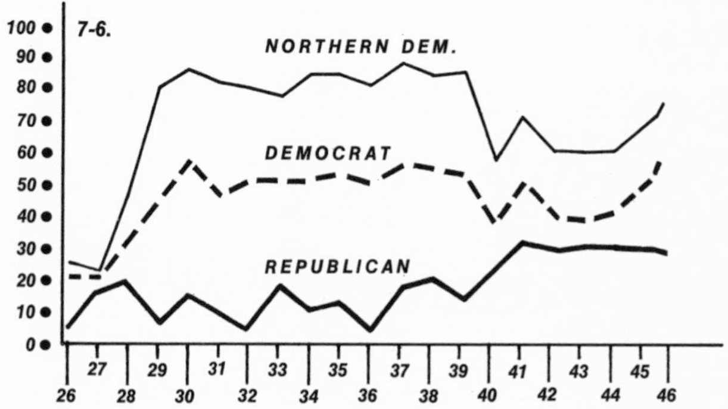

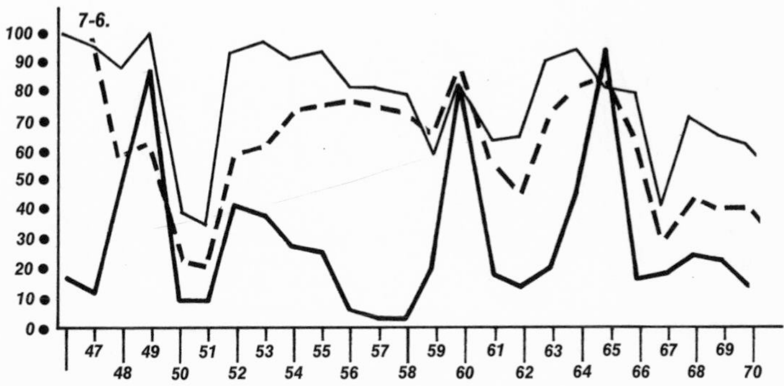

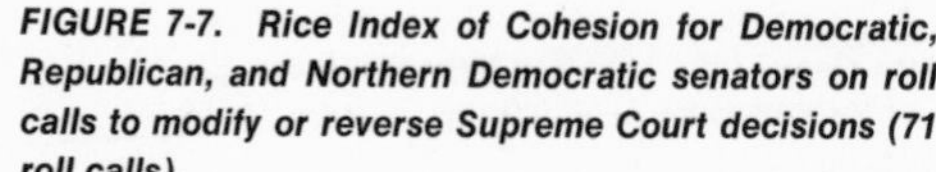

FIGURE 7-7. Rice Index of Cohesion for Democratic, Republican, and Northern Democratic senators on roll calls to modify or reverse Supreme Court decisions (71 roll calls).

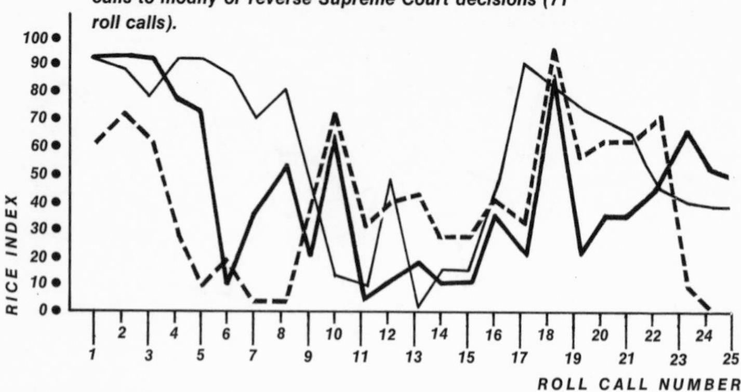

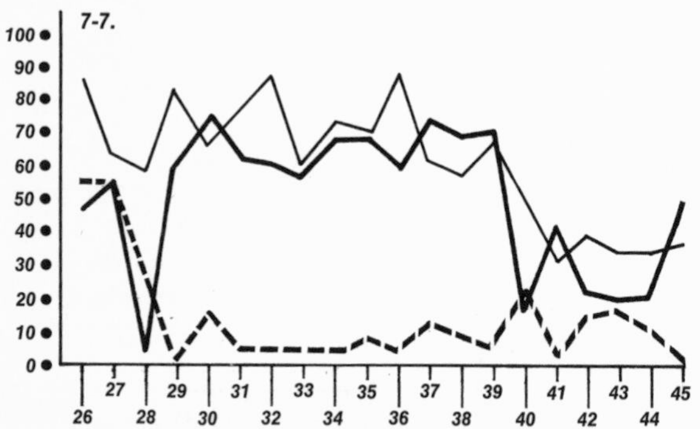

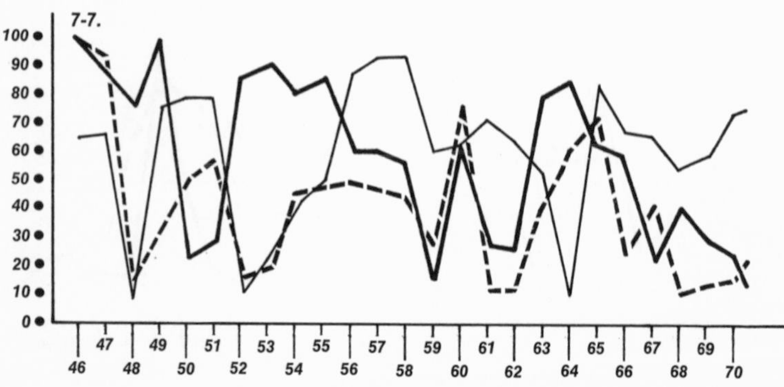

TABLE 7-5. *Average percentage of Democratic, Republican, and Southern and Northern Democratic representatives supporting the Supreme Court on roll calls to modify or reverse Supreme Court decisions, 80th through 90th Congresses.*

	Party			
	Dem.	Rep.	N. Dem.	S. Dem.
Average percentage (35 roll calls)	48.1	13.0	65.3	16.5

TABLE 7-6. *Rice Index of Cohesion for Democratic, Republican, and Southern and Northern Democratic representatives on roll calls to reverse or modify Supreme Court decisions, 80th through 90th Congresses.*

	Party			
	Dem.	Rep.	N. Dem.	S. Dem.
Rice Index (35 roll calls)	23.1	70.0	42.2	76.0

TABLE 7-7. *Average percentage of Democratic, Republican, and Southern and Northern Democratic senators supporting the Supreme Court on roll calls attempting to modify or reverse Supreme Court decisions, 80th through 90th Congresses.*

	Party			
	Dem.	Rep.	N. Dem.	S. Dem.
Average percentage (71 roll calls)	55.4	24.2	72.3	33.5

TABLE 7-8. *Rice Index of Cohesion for Democratic, Republican, and Southern and Northern Democratic senators on roll calls modifying or reversing Supreme Court decisions, 80th through 90th Congresses.*

	Party			
	Dem.	Rep.	N. Dem.	S. Dem.
Rice Index (71 roll calls)	33.4	60.6	59.3	69.6

classification. But it is interesting to note that the differences are not great except for the Northern Democrats. 55.4% of all Democrats supported the Court against direct institutional attacks while 48.1% supported it against Congressional statutory reversals. 19.2% of the Republicans supported the Court against direct attacks and 13% supported it against statutory reversals. But 82.3% of the Northern Democrats supported the Court against direct institutional attacks while 65.3% supported it against Congressional statutory reversals. It is clear, therefore, that the distinction between types of anti-Court actions is far more meaningful to Northern Democrats than it is to those congressmen who may comprise the Conservative Coalition. The data for the senators indicate a similar pattern. Support by every classification of senator is stronger for the Supreme Court in divisions involving direct institutional attacks. But Senate Republicans gave stronger support in both issue categories and Northern Democratic senators did not make as sharp a distinction between the types of roll calls. Thus 60% of all Democratic senators supported the Court against direct institutional attacks in contrast to 55.4% against ordinary reversals. A higher percentage of Senate Republicans (37.3%) opposed institutional attacks than House Republicans (19.2%), and 24.2% of the Republican senators opposed reversals. Eighty-three percent of the Senate Democrats supported the Court against direct attacks (a percentage virtually identical to the House Democrats' 82.3%), while they supported the Court on statutory reversals (72.3%) better than their House counterparts (at 65.3%).

CONCLUSION

The foregoing summary of preliminary research indicates that the voting behavior of members of Congress on Court-related roll calls is basically similar to their over-all voting tendencies. Jewell and Patterson summed up the findings on party differences and party cohesion in 1966 as follows:

> The few studies available indicate that the Democratic congressmen who vote most consistently with the party have been those from Northern metropolitan districts, with a high proportion of foreign-born or (in more recent years) non-white population. Rural Republicans are likely to have a more loyal voting record than those who represent the kind of metropolitan distrust that usually votes Democratic.[74]

[74] Jewell and Patterson, *op. cit.*, p. 437.

Basic to most scholarly evaluations of Congress-Court relations has been the assumption that congressmen view the Court as a hallowed institution. If this assumption is valid, then the members of Congress presumably will treat Court-related issues differently than non-judicial issues and will vote in a manner that reflects special attention to the Court as an institution. Some political scientists have accorded a particularly reverential role to lawyer-legislators, apparently on the assumption that the professional socialization of lawyers in some way contributed to the development of such an institutional attitude.

The preliminary evidence simply does not support the first of these assumptions. The partisan and regional divisions in Court-related roll calls are not substantially different from the general voting behavior of members of Congress. The evidence therefore, does not support the "reverence for the Court" hypothesis. Our initial investigation of the hypothesis with respect to lawyer-legislators utilized all the Court-related roll calls voted upon in the Senate, 2nd Session, 79th Congress. Four separate votes, all involving reversal of statutory interpretation issues comprised the total. The percentage of lawyer-legislators and non-lawyer legislators supporting or opposing the Supreme Court is summarized for each consecutive roll call in Table 7-9. The results not only fail to support the "lawyers' reverence" hypothesis, but contradict it. In only one roll call is the percentage of lawyer-legislators supporting the Court higher

TABLE 7-9. *Senatorial lawyer and non-lawyer support for the Supreme Court, 2nd Session, 79th Congress, by percentage.*

	Lawyer	Non-Lawyer
	Roll Call 3	
Pro-Court	27%	36%
Anti-Court	71%	60%
	Roll Call 4	
Pro-Court	43%	46%
Anti-Court	57%	54%
	Roll Call 5	
Pro-Court	39%	39%
Anti-Court	61%	61%
	Roll Call 6	
Pro-Court	44%	39%
Anti-Court	52%	61%

(by a slight margin) than that of the non-lawyer legislators. In two roll calls the reverse is true, while in the third the percentages are identical.

Finally, for preliminary exploratory purposes, we utilized regression and factor analysis to help identify the variable or variables that might explain Congressional roll-call behavior vis-à-vis the Supreme Court. The universe of votes comprised all of the roll calls (numbers 1 through 7) cast in the House and Senate in the first and second sessions of the 79th Congress. In accordance with a multitude of previous Congressional roll call studies, we hypothesized that support or non-support (as measured by yeas and nays on pro- or anti-Court roll calls) of the Supreme Court may be related to one or more of six factors. These independent variables are (1) party affiliation, (2) region, (3) legal professionalism, (4) elective legislative leadership role, (5) seniority ranking, and (6) membership on the Senate or House Judiciary Committee.

The first roll call considered was House Resolution 60, a joint resolution proposing an amendment to the Constitution concerning the treaty-making power. Table 7-10 clearly demonstrates that the relationship between the independent variables and the dependent variable is very slight. All of the independent variables account for a multiple R of .24602 and a coefficient of multiple determination (r^2) of 6 per cent. Party affiliation is correlated with the roll call at the $-.218$ level with an R of .0422, which is statistically significant at the .01 level. The other independent variables account for very little variance reduction, and party affiliation obviously fails to account for much.

Table 7-11 contains the results of the regression analysis for the roll-call vote on a provision for an appeal to the Supreme Court of a decision of the U.S. Court of Claims in a suit by Georgia. Again very little variance is explained by the independent variables. However, in addition to party affiliation, the lawyer/nonlawyer and Judiciary Committee variables evidence some association, although the association is low indeed. Both the lawyer and the Judiciary Committee variables, moreover, account for less than 1 per cent of the total variance.

The second session of the 79th Congress was marked, for our purposes, by the Tidelands Oil issue. The one House roll call of interest deals with an attempt to override the President's veto of an anti-Court bill.

TABLE 7-10. *Multiple correlation coefficients of roll-call vote variables: H.R. 60.*

	Region	Party	Lawyer	Elective Leadership	Seniority	Judiciary Committee	Roll call	R	F
Region	—	.296	.055	.006	.057	.042	.068	.0001	.0215
Party	.296	—	.123	.165	.008	.008	.218	.0422	17.2736
Lawyer Code	.055	−.123	—	.003	.042	.200	.081	.0044	1.9358
Elective Leadership	.006	−.165	.003	—	.052	.056	.061	.0004	.1839
Seniority	.057	−.008	.042	.052	—	.034	.088	.0086	3.9878
Judiciary Committee	0.42	−.008	.200	.056	−.034	—	.016	.0011	.4701
Roll Call	.068	−.218	.081	.061	−.088	−0.16	—		

Multiple R = .24602
Coefficient of multiple determination (r^2) = 6 per cent
df = 440

TABLE 7-11. *Multiple Correlation coefficients of roll-call vote variables: Jurisdictional controversy re U.S. Court of Claims.*

	I	II	III	IV	V	VI	VII	R	F
Region I	—	.296	.055	.006	.057	.042	.050	.005	.22278
Party II	−.296	—	.123	.165	.008	.008	.128	.0113	4.6586
Lawyers Code III	.055	−.123	—	.003	.042	.200	.106	.0022	.9727
Elective Leadership IV	.006	−.165	.003	—	.052	.056	.051	.0022	.9997
Seniority Leadership Code V	.057	−.008	.042	−.052	—	.034	.022	.008	.3582
Judiciary Committee VI	−.042	−.008	.200	−.056	−.034	—	.222	.0470	21.1893
Roll Call VII	.050	−.128	.106	.051	.022	.222	—		

Multiple R = .26626
Coefficient of multiple determination (r^2) = 7 per cent
df = 440

TABLE 7-12. *Multiple correlation coefficients of roll-call vote variables: Vote to override presidential veto of Tidelands Oil Bill.*

	I	II	III	IV	V	VI	VII	R	R
Region	—	.308	.068	.016	.007	−.043	−.082	.0019	.9041
Party	−.308	—	.119	−.158	.014	−.009	.401	.1732	80.0288
Lawyers Code	.068	−.119	—	.001	.031	.216	.024	.0041	2.0300
Elective Leadership	.016	−.158	.001	—	−.041	.059	−.103	.0013	.6709
Seniority Leadership	.007	.014	.031	−.040	—	−.059	.017	.0001	.0410
Judiciary	−.043	−.009	.216	−.059	−.059	—	.036	.0007	.3553
Roll Call	−.082	.401	.024	−.103	.017	.036	—		

Multiple R = .41179
r^2 = 17 per cent
df = 440

TABLE 7-13. *Multiple correlation coefficients of roll-call vote variables: Vote on provisions of Tidelands Oil Bill.*

	I	II	III	IV	V	VI	VII
Region I	—	−.317	.091	.051	−.064	.218	.063
Party II	−.317	—	−.188	.053	−.122	−.054	.204
Lawyer III	.091	−.188	—	.278	.218	.398	.068
Elective Leadership IV	.051	−.053	.278	—	.239	.140	−.002
Seniority V	−.064	−.122	.218	.239	—	−.005	.039
Judiciary Committee VI	.218	−.054	.398	.140	−.005	—	.061
Roll Calls VII	.063	.204	.068	−.002	.039	.061	—

Multiple R = .27454
Coefficient of multiple determination (r^2) = 7 per cent
df = 440

As Table 7-12 clearly demonstrates, party affiliation is the most important independent variable. It contributed nearly all the explained variance reduction.

The second session of the 79th Congress had several roll calls dealing with the Tidelands Oil issue. The Senate voted on four roll calls on the Tidelands Oil issue. Through the use of factor analysis a composite score for each senator was obtained. This score was then utilized as the dependent variable in the regression equation. Not surprisingly, the results in Table 7-13 are similar to our other findings. Again, the only association of any strength is party affiliation. Moreover, the total variance explained is only 7 per cent.[75] It must be concluded on the basis of the findings that none of the variables, either individually or collectively, adequately explains roll-call behavior. Although party affiliation consistently correlates with roll-call behavior, the association is generally small and accounts for very little variance reduction. As far the basic assumptions often made about Congressional reverence for the Court and lawyer-legislator concern for judicial institutions, the preliminary investigation does not support these hypotheses. Yet, the results do not clearly indicate positive alternative explanations, although partisanship tentatively emerges as the most appropriate alternative. The stability of Conservative Coalition opposition to the Supreme Court especially warrants further investigation.

THE PUBLIC POLICY IMPLICATIONS OF THE ROLL-CALL INVESTIGATION

One of the most explicit contemporary summations of conventional wisdom regarding Congressional behavior toward the Supreme Court was provided by an analyst for the *Christian Science Monitor*. He commented about the controversies raging around the Warren Court:

> Most lawmakers appear to expect that, as before, an indefined sense of congressional tolerance will provide the bridge. . . . even

[75] The percentages were derived through utilization of the Nucros program for multivariate cross-classification developed by Professor Kenneth Janda of Northwestern University and adapted for the Political Research Laboratory, University of Iowa, by Merle Wood. Kenneth Janda, *Data Processing* (Evanston: Northwestern University Press, 1969), pp. 153–168, especially, pp. 161–167.

> when Congress has given vent to the noisiest complaints about the court by the constituents back home, the lawmakers have kept an attitude of near reverence for the court's standing as the ultimate constitutional arbiter. . . .[76]

The investigation of Court-oriented voting divisions in the period from 1945 to 1968 suggests that partisan and ideological considerations play a far greater role in Congressional behavior toward the Court. The persistence and relative growth of Conservative Coalition antagonism toward the Supreme Court does not bode well for the judicial institution in the immediate future. Since 1969, the presence of a President who has often associated himself with the Conservative Coalition on issues involving crime, procedural due process, and judicial nominations has compounded the seriousness of the Supreme Court's position. In short, the Supreme Court as an institution as well as the fate of its policy directions through the Warren years may be in more serious trouble than many have believed. A curious overdependence upon an alleged Congressional attitude of "reverence" for the Court has compounded the difficulty by masking the significance of the Court's persistent modern opposition.

[76] "Congress v. the Court," *Christian Science Monitor* (2nd Section), July 18, 1969, p. 9.

INDEX

Index